NA1392-7

C0-APX-948

GEORGE E. MAYCOCK

GOD AND HIS CHURCH

A Scripture Guide

by

Duane S. Crowther

HORIZON
PUBLISHERS

191 North 650 East
Bountiful, Utah 84010

"Continue thou in the things which thou hast learned and hast been assured of, knowing of whom thou hast learned them;

And that from a child thou hast known the holy scriptures, which are able to make thee wise unto salvation through faith which is in Christ Jesus.

All scripture is given by inspiration of God, and is profitable for doctrine, for reproof, for correction, for instruction in righteousness:

That the man of God may be perfect, throughly furnished unto all good works."

(2 Timothy 3:14-17)

Companion volumes to this scripture guide are

THE PLAN OF SALVATION
and
THE FUTURE IN PROPHECY

COME UNTO CHRIST

A GUIDE TO EFFECTIVE SCRIPTURE STUDY

Available at L.D.S. bookstores or
order direct from

HORIZON PUBLISHERS
191 North 650 East
Bountiful, Utah 84010

TABLE OF CONTENTS

Working in the Church

Missionary Work

Contents of Companion Volumes

INTRODUCTION

How to Use This Book

God and His Church is a pocket scripture guide designed to be of value to all who study and love the revealed word of God. Together with its companion volumes, *The Plan of Salvation and The Future in Prophecy, Come Unto Christ,* and *A Guide to Effective Scripture Study,* it offers a comprehensive coverage of the major doctrines of The Church of Jesus Christ of Latter-day Saints. Passages are included from the Bible, the Book of Mormon, the Doctrine and Covenants, and the Pearl of Great Price.

Study of the scriptures is the basic preparation man must make to serve effectively in the kingdom of God. This book is designed to aid in that endeavor in four ways:

1. It is a *pocket reference volume* which lists the most important scriptural passages on many related subjects. These passages have been carefully selected as being those which have the greatest value and use for talks, classes, missionary conversations, and personal gospel study. The passages are presented in a comprehensive manner, with careful indexing provided for the four-volume series in *A Guide To Effective Scripture Study.* Numerous subjects are included in the series which are not found in other scripture lists.

This book is made to fit conveniently into a pocket or to be carried with a missionary Bible or triple combination. Many missionaries carry it in a plastic zipper cover similar to the ones on their standard works.

2. It is a *study guide.* The passages are carefully cross-referenced to other related scriptures. Many of the listings are correlated with in-depth discussions of the topics in other Church works and with pertinent listings in the companion volumes in this series. By carefully following the related references, most of the major teachings of the gospel will be systematically considered.

3. It is a series of *talk and lesson outlines.* The passages for each topic are arranged in order so that the first five, six, or seven scriptures in each section form a meaningful outline for a sermon or teaching presentation. This can be an important aid, especially in unexpected situations where one is required to speak or teach extemporaneously. Space is also provided so the user may renumber the scriptures to suit his own order of presentation if he wishes.

4. It is a *scripture memorization program.* For a thorough knowledge of the scriptures, there is no substitute for a systematic memorization plan. To aid in memorization, most of the passages listed are short and concise. Ten passages are listed in each section or subject area, but it is suggested that those memorizing a scripture each day choose seven and then move to the next topic so that a new subject is studied each week. At this rate, fourteen sections, or approximately one hundred passages, will be learned in four months, with time allowed for review. A highly effective memorization program is provided in *A Guide To Effective Scripture Study,*

the index volume for the series. Its use is strongly recommended to those who are beginning a memorization program. In addition to indexing all of the passages in the four companion volumes, it provides record-keeping forms, short- and long-range goals, and many valuable suggestions on how to memorize effectively.

Basis for Choice of Passages

The guidelines which have governed the selection of passages for this volume are:

1. The passages must be judged the *most suitable*. Many scripture reference books list numerous references without making any value judgment as to their usability. In this volume, a careful weighing of each passage has taken place in order to choose those passages which are *most* useful. While this is a matter of personal opinion, the reader will still find almost every passage to be vital to the subject under consideration and a useable addition to his knowledge.

2. They must be *varied*. Rather than choosing ten passages which say the same thing, the author has selected a variety of scriptures which introduce various aspects of the subject.

3. They must be *readable*. Many passages have been excluded because they have complicated, involved phraseology which makes them hard to understand when used in talks and lessons. In some cases such passages have been adapted by omitting irrelevant phrases and by dropping introductory words such as "verily I say unto you," "and it came to pass," "behold," "yea," "now," "and," etc. When

such exclusions have been made proper indication has been made in the text.

4. They must be *easily understood.*

5. They must be *pertinent.*

6. Some must be *new.* The continual use of the same passages causes them to become trite and less effective, just as takes place with the overuse of any other expression of speech. An effort has been made to incorporate meaningful passages which are less known. Many of the passages in this companion series are not listed in the scripture reference books which have previously been available. The program found in the four companion volumes is far broader and embraces many pertinent subjects untreated in other reference volumes.

7. They must be *short.* The goal has been to list key passages which are easily learned.

Terms and Symbols Used

Several terms and symbols have been employed in this volume and should be defined to those who use it. They include

1. *Section* - Each section is a subject topic and is listed in the table of contents.

2. *Scripture number* - Every passage has a number, which is listed to the left of the reference in bold type. In the series index, passages will be listed in this style **A 12 2**, meaning volume A, section 12, scripture number 2.

3. *Situation* - Nearly every passage is followed by the abbreviation *SIT.* which introduces a brief explanation of its background and related circum-

stances. This material is useful in explaining the context to others.

4. *Context* - Some passages are followed by the abbreviation *CON.:* and a scriptural reference. This is a marking aid which indicates the full extent of the story setting or doctrinal theme.

5. *Cross Reference* - The abbreviation *C.R.:* is frequently used to introduce other pertinent references which should be marked in the margin by the scripture. Some references will be preceded by a parallel mark (=), which indicates that the reference is another account of the same event or is a similar revelation using substantially the same wording.

6. *Use* - In a few cases, where the proper application for a passage may not be apparent, the word *USE* is used to introduce a suggestion for the application of the passage.

7. *Note* - This term is used to introduce words of caution, explanation, or emphasis.

8. *Square Brackets* - In a few passages an additional word or phrase is introduced with square brackets: ($\boxed{}$) These words should be learned as part of the passage, yet an awareness that these words have been inserted for clarity or readability should be maintained. Even though they are not a part of the passage itself, in every case they are clearly implied in the context of the passage. Their use is justified on the basis of simplicity and clarity.

9. *Curved brackets* - These have been placed to the left of each reference. This space can be used to renumber the order of the passages or for checking as the passages are studied and/or memorized.

10. *Large bracket* - Some lengthy passages have been broken into several short passages for ease in use and memorization. A large square bracket placed in the left margin is used to show that they are all part of the same passage. Only one set of explanatory notes is used in such cases. It will be found following the last passage in the bracket.

11. *Ellipsis periods* - In some cases phrases not pertinent to the topic have been omitted from passages. In these instances the omission is indicated by three dots (...). Always check the passage in the standard works and be aware of what has been left out.

Related Study Sources

At the end of many of the sections, cross references to other works by the author are listed. These books include:

Prophecy—Key to the Future (Salt Lake City, Utah: Bookcraft, Inc., 1962), 355 pp., appendices, bibliography, indexes, extensively documented. This book is adapted from a masters thesis written for and accepted by the Department of Bible and Modern Scripture at Brigham Young University. The objective of the book is to present and document a chronology of the future based on prophecies found in the scriptures and prophecies made by L.D.S. General Authorities. The chapters treat numerous events including a third world war, internal wars and the collapse of U.S. government, the establishment of the political kingdom of God, the New Jerusalem, the gathering of Israel, four appearances of Christ, the battle of Armageddon, Christ's coming in glory, the millenium, the earth's final state, etc.

The Prophecies of Joseph Smith (Salt Lake City, Utah: Bookcraft, 1963), 413 pp., appendices, index, extensively documented. This volume examines and analyzes 365 prophetic items and their fulfillment, reports many interesting supernatural events which occurred during the ministry of Joseph Smith, and contains an outline and atlas of his life. This is an ideal book for investigators, new members, students of Church history, and all seeking a testimony of the divine origin of the L.D.S. Church.

Gifts of the Spirit (Salt Lake City, Utah: Bookcraft, 1965), 352 pp., indexes, extensively documented. In this work, an analysis of the workings of the Holy Ghost is made. Suggestions for effective seeking of the Spirit are made and aids in recognizing His promptings are given. Twenty-six spiritual gifts are analyzed. This book records hundreds of personal spiritual manifestations drawn from histories, diaries, and other sources. It is a valuable aid to all who seek inspiration and divine guidance.

Prophets and Prophecies of the Old Testament (Salt Lake City, Utah: Deseret Book Company, 1966), 644 pp., index, colored map section. This book presents each of the Old Testament prophetic and historical books in an understandable and usable outline and summary form. Numerous doctrinal and historical notes provide understanding in difficult areas. Extensive suggestions concerning how to study and interpret scripture, plus aids for understanding Bible history and chronology are given. Passages related to the six major doctrines of the Old Testament prophets are listed. The book is one of the most usable Bible handbooks about the Old Testament prophets available.

Life Everlasting (Salt Lake City, Utah: Bookcraft, 1967), 399 pp., bibliography, indexes, extensively documented. This book studies death and life after death using the scriptures, statements by L.D.S. General Authorities, and numerous historical spirit world experiences as its basis. Chapters consider topics including death, paradise, hell, missionary work in the spirit prison, the resurrection, the final judgment, the sons of perdition, the degrees of glory, and exaltation. This book provides substantial evidence and new insights on many of life's most profound questions.

1. REVELATION AND SCRIPTURE

( ) **1. Amos 3:7**

Surely the Lord God will do nothing, but he reveal-eth his secret unto his servants the prophets.
> *SIT.: These words were spoken by Amos as he attempted to show the children of Israel that they must walk in agreement with their Lord. CON.: Amos 3:1-8. C.R.: Hos. 12:19; Is. 45:11-13; Jer. 33:3; Dan. 2:20-22, 28, 45.*

( ) **2. D & C 1:38**

What I the Lord have spoken, I have spoken, and I excuse not myself; and though the heavens and the earth pass away, my word shall not pass away, but shall all be fulfilled, whether by mine own voice or by the voice of my servants, it is the same.
> *SIT.: This revelation was given through Joseph Smith to elders of the church in 1831. CON.: D & C 1:24-28, 37-39.*

( ) **3. 2 Pet. 1:20-21**

No prophecy of the scripture is of any private inter-pretation. For the prophecy came not in old time by the will of man: but holy men of God spake as they were moved by the Holy Ghost.
> *CON.: 1 Pet. 1:19-21. USE: Use with Gen. 40:8. Just as prophecies are revealed through the Holy Ghost, the interpretation must also be revealed through the Holy Ghost. C.R.: 1 Cor. 14:32; Moro. 10:5.*

( ) 4. 3 Ne. 29:6

Wo unto him that shall deny the revelations of the
Lord, and that shall say the Lord no longer worketh
by revelation, or by prophecy, or by gifts, or by
tongues, or by healings, or by the power of the Holy
Ghost!

> *SIT.: Mormon's warning is written to the Gentiles
> who will read the Book of Mormon in the last days.*
> CON.: 3 Ne. 29:1-9.

( ) 5. Prov. 29:18

Where there is no vision, the people perish.

( ) 6. Moro. 10:4

When ye shall receive these things, I would exhort
you that ye would ask God, the Eternal Father, in the
name of Christ, if these things are not true; and if ye
shall ask with a sincere heart, with real intent, having faith in Christ, he will manifest the truth of it
unto you, by the power of the Holy Ghost.

> *SIT.: Moroni is writing to the Lamanites who are
> to receive the Book of Mormon in the last days.*
> CON.: Moro. 10:1-5.

( ) 7. D & C 93:24-25

Truth is knowledge of things as they are, and as
they were, and as they are to come; And whatsoever
is more or less than this is the spirit of that wicked
one who was a liar from the beginning.

> *SIT.: This revelation was given to the church
> through Joseph Smith in 1833.* CON.: D & C
> 93:23-38.

( ) **8. 2 Ne. 29:3**

Because my words shall hiss forth—many of the Gentiles shall say: A Bible! A Bible! We have got a Bible, and there cannot be any more Bible.

   SIT.: Nephi is prophesying the reaction of many of the Gentiles to the Book of Mormon when it comes forth. CON.: 2 Ne. 29:3-14.

( ) **9. Eccles. 12:12**

Of making many books there is no end.

   SIT.: The preacher had been seeking to learn what would bring man happiness. Though he knew that study was tiresome, yet he knew that the words of the wise would be continually written and preserved. CON.: Eccles. 12:9-14. USE: Does the context indicate that these books are new scripture?

( ) **10. Heb. 13:8**

Jesus Christ the same yesterday, and to day, and for ever.

   USE: If the Lord is unchangeable, and chose to reveal his will in one age, then he will also reveal his will in other dispensations. C.R.: Mal. 3:6; Jas. 1:17.

See "God's Communication With Man," *Prophets and Prophecies of The Old Testament,* pp. 80-83, for an extensive listing of passages pertaining to the prophetic function and the nature of revelation and prophecy.

2. STUDY SCRIPTURE

( ) 1. **D & C 84:85**

Treasure up in your minds continually the words of life, and it shall be given you in the very hour that portion that shall be meted unto every man.

    C.R.: Mt. 10:18-20; D & C 100:5-8.

( ) 2. **D & C 41:12**

These words are given unto you, and they are pure before me; wherefore, beware how you hold them, for they are to be answered upon your souls in the day of judgment.

( ) 3. **D & C 26:1**

Let your time be devoted to the studying of the scriptures, and to preaching, and to confirming the church.

    SIT.: This revelation was given to Joseph Smith, Oliver Cowdery, and John Whitmer. USE: By example.

( ) 4. **Deut. 17:19**

The law of God shall be with him, and he shall read therein all the days of his life: that he may learn to fear the LORD his God, to keep all the words of this law and these statutes, to do them.

    SIT.: The Lord revealed that this would be a requirement for whoever would be chosen to lead Israel. CON.: Deut. 17:14-20.

( ) **5. Ps. 1:2**

His delight is in the law of the LORD; and in his law doth he meditate day and night.
SIT.: This is a portion of the psalmist's description of a righteous man.

( ) **6. Acts 17:11-12**

They received the word with all readiness of mind, and searched the scriptures daily, whether those things were so. Therefore many of them believed.
SIT.: This is Luke's description of the saints and investigators in Berea.

( ) **7. Jn. 5:39**

Search the scriptures; for in them ye think ye have eternal life: and they are they which testify of me.
SIT.: This was Jesus' challenge to a group of unbelieving Jews. CON.: Jn. 5:18-47.

( ) **8. 1 Ne. 19:23**

I did liken all scriptures unto us, that it might be for our profit and learning.
SIT.: This was Nephi's explanation of his method of scriptural study. CON.: 1 Ne. 19:22-24.

( ) **9. 3 Ne. 23:1, 3**

A commandment I give unto you that ye search these things diligently; for great are the words of Isaiah... And all things that he spake have been and shall be, even according to the words which he spake.

SIT.: Jesus gave this commandment to the Lamanites and Nephites to whom he appeared in the Americas following his resurrection. C.R.: 1 Ne. 19:23; 2 Ne. 11:2; 2 Ne. 25:1, 4, 7; 3 Ne. 20:11-12; 1 Ne. 15:20; Morm. 8:23.

( ) 10. 2 Ne. 9:4

I know that ye have searched much, many of you, to know of things to come...

SIT.: This was the prophet Jacob's acknowledgment of the scriptural study of the people of Nephi.

See "How To Study and Interpret Scripture," *Prophets and Prophecies of The Old Testament*, pp. 15-35.

3. PURPOSES OF SCRIPTURE

( ) **1. D & C 35:20**

The scriptures shall be given, even as they are in mine own bosom, to the salvation of mine own elect.
SIT.: This statement was made by the Lord in a revelation given through Joseph Smith to Sidney Rigdon, in which Sidney was commanded to serve as scribe to Joseph Smith. CON.: D & C 35:3-23.

( ) **2. Ro. 15:4**

Whatsoever things were written aforetime were written for our learning, that we through patience and comfort of the scriptures might have hope.

( ) **3. 2 Tim. 3:15**

From a child thou hast known the holy scriptures, which are able to make thee wise unto salvation through faith which is in Christ Jesus.

( ) **4. 2 Tim. 3:16**

All scripture is given by inspiration of God, and is profitable for doctrine, for reproof, for correction, for instruction in righteousness.

( ) **5. JS 1:37**

Whoso treasureth up my word, shall not be deceived.

( ) **6. D & C 33:16**

The Book of Mormon and the holy scriptures are given of me for your instruction; and the power of my Spirit quickeneth all things.

SIT.: This revelation was given through Joseph Smith to Ezra Thayre and Northrop Sweet in 1830.

( ) **7. Josh. 1:8**

This book of the law shall not depart out of thy mouth; but thou shalt meditate therein day and night, that thou mayest observe to do according to all that is written therein: for then thou shalt make thy way prosperous, and then thou shalt have good success.

SIT.: This was a commandment which the Lord gave to Joshua as he assumed leadership of the Israelites and prepared to lead them into the promised land.

( ) **8. D & C 52:14**

I will give unto you a pattern in all things, that ye may not be deceived; for Satan is abroad in the land, and he goeth forth deceiving the nations.

( ) **9. 1 Pet. 2:2-3**

As newborn babes, desire the sincere milk of the word, that ye may grow thereby: If so be ye have tasted that the Lord is gracious.

( ) **10. D & C 1:24-26**

These commandments are of me, and were given unto my servants in their weakness, after the manner of their language, that they might come to understanding. And inasmuch as they erred it might be made known; And inasmuch as they sought wisdom they might be instructed.

C.R.: 2 Ne. 31:2-3; 25:4, 7-8; Jac. 4:13.

See "The Gift of Expounding the Scriptures," *Gifts of the Spirit,* pp. 262-268.

4. THE STANDARD WORKS

A knowledge of the names and order of the books of the scriptures of the church is essential to all who wish to study the scriptures efficiently. These books are presented below in groups to aid in their memorization. It is recommended that the diacritical marks given in the scriptures be consulted so that proper pronunciation is learned. Most good Bibles indicate the pronunciation for proper names wherever the names occur. The pronunciation for each book is usually found in the first several verses of the book. A pronouncing vocabulary is provided on pages 531-534 of current editions of the Book of Mormon. The abbreviations for the scriptural books should also be studied.

1. Books of the New Testament:

A.	Matthew	Mt.
	Mark	Mk.
	Luke	Lk.
	John	Jn.
B.	Acts	Acts
	Romans	Ro.
	First Corinthians	1 Cor.
	Second Corinthians	2 Cor.
C.	Galatians	Gal.
	Ephesians	Eph.
	Philippians	Phil.
	Colossians	Col.

D. First Thessalonians   1 Thess.
    Second Thessalonians   2 Thess.
    First Timothy   1 Tim.
    Second Timothy   2 Tim.

E. Titus   Tit.
    Philemon   Philem.
    Hebrews   Heb.
    James   Jas.

F. First Peter   1 Pet.
    Second Peter   2 Pet.
    First John   1 Jn.
    Second John   2 Jn.
    Third John   3 Jn.

G. Jude   Jude
    Revelation   Rev.

2. Books of the Old Testament:

A. Genesis   Gen.
    Exodus   Ex.
    Leviticus   Lev.
    Numbers   Num.
    Deuteronomy   Deut.

B. Joshua   Josh.
    Judges   Judg.
    Ruth   Ruth

C. First Samuel   1 Sam.
    Second Samuel   2 Sam.
    First Kings   1 Ki.
    Second Kings   2 Ki.
    First Chronicles   1 Chron.
    Second Chronicles   2 Chron.

D. Ezra	Ezra
Nehemiah	Neh.
Esther	Esther
E. Job	Job
Psalms	Ps.
Proverbs	Prov.
Ecclesiastes	Eccles.
Song of Solomon	Song.
F. Isaiah	Is.
Jeremiah	Jer.
Lamentations	Lam.
G. Ezekiel	Ezek.
Daniel	Dan.
Hosea	Hos.
H. Joel	Joel
Amos	Amos
Obadiah	Obad.
I. Jonah	Jon.
Micah	Mi.
Nahum	Nahum
J. Habakkuk	Hab.
Zephaniah	Zeph.
Haggai	Hag.
K. Zechariah	Zech.
Malachi	Mal.

3. Books of the Book of Mormon: (B. of M.)

A. First Nephi	1 Ne.
Second Nephi	2 Ne.

B. Jacob	Jac.
Enos	Enos
Jarom	Jar.
Omni	Om.
Words of Mormon	W. of Morm.
C. Mosiah	Mos.
Alma	Al.
Helaman	He.
D. Third Nephi	3 Ne.
Fourth Nephi	4 Ne.
E. Mormon	Morm.
Ether	Eth.
Moroni	Moro.

4. Books of the Pearl of Great Price: (P. of G.P.)

Moses	Moses
Abraham	Abra.
Joseph Smith One	JS 1
Joseph Smith Two	JS 2
Articles of Faith	A of F

5. The Doctrine and Covenants (D & C)

136 sections and the Official Declaration (Manifesto concerning the end of plural marriage)

D & C 21:3 means Doctrine and Covenants section twenty-one, verse three.

5. FATHER AND SON HAVE TANGIBLE BODIES

( ) **1. Jn. 17:3**

This is life eternal, that they might know thee the
only true God, and Jesus Christ, whom thou hast
sent.

*SIT.: Jesus spoke these words in a prayer to his
Father on the Mt. of Olives shortly before his
betrayal. It was witnessed by his disciples, to
whom he had previously explained man's relationship to God. CON.: Jn. 15-17. USE: This
passage is used to establish the need for man to
understand the true nature of God.*

( ) **2. Lk. 24:39**

Behold my hands and my feet, that it is I myself:
handle me, and see; for a spirit hath not flesh and
bones, as ye see me have.

*SIT.: Jesus spoke these words to his disciples
as he appeared to them following his resurrection.
USE: To show that resurrected beings are physical beings and not just spirits. CON.: Lk.
24:36-49. C.R.: Jn. 20:19-29; Mk. 16:14; 3 Ne.
11:14-17.*

( ) **3. Jn. 20:27**

Reach hither thy finger, and behold my hands; and
reach hither thy hand, and thrust it into my side:
and be not faithless, but believing.

*SIT.: These words were spoken by Jesus to
Thomas, who was absent when the resurrected*

Lord appeared to his apostles a week earlier, and who had said he would not believe unless he could see Christ's wounds. CON.: Jn. 20:24-29. NOTE: Thomas should not always be considered in the role of the doubter, for he had great faith; see Jn. 11:16. C.R.: 3 Ne. 11:14-17; D & C 45:48-52; Zech. 13:6.

( ) **4. Ro. 6:9**

Christ being raised from the dead dieth no more; death hath no more dominion over him.

SIT.: Paul is comparing baptism to Christ's death and resurrection. USE: To show that once a spirit and body have been reunited to become a resurrected being, they cannot be separated again. C.R.: Jas. 2:26; Lk. 20:36.

( ) **5. Acts 1:11**

Ye men of Galilee, why stand ye gazing up into heaven? this same Jesus, which is taken up from you into heaven, shall so come in like manner as ye have seen him go into heaven.

SIT.: These words were spoken by two messengers who appeared to the disciples as Christ ascended into heaven. USE: To show that Christ, who went into heaven with his body, will still have it when he returns in glory. CON.: Acts 1:2-11. C.R.: 1 Jn. 3:2.

( ) **6. 1 Jn. 3:2**

Beloved, now are we the sons of God, and it doth

not yet appear what we shall be: but we know that, when he shall appear, we shall be like him; for we shall see him as he is.

USE: To show that Christ's resurrected body will appear like man's when he comes in glory. C.R.: Acts 1:11.

( ) 7. D & C 130:22

The Father has a body of flesh and bones as tangible as man's; the Son also; but the Holy Ghost has not a body of flesh and bones, but is a personage of Spirit. Were it not so, the Holy Ghost could not dwell in us.

USE: This is the basic scriptural statement of the nature of the Godhead. C.R.: D & C 131:7-8.

( ) 8. Gen. 1:26-27

God said, Let us make man in our image, after our likeness:...So God created man in his own image, in the image of God created he him; male and female created he them.

USE: Man, with his physical body, is created in the image of God. God, therefore, must also have a physical body. , C.R.: =Abra. 4:26-27; =Moses 2:26-28; D & C 20:17-18; Gen. 5:1-3.

( ) 9. Gen. 32:30

Jacob called the name of the place Peniel: for I have seen God face to face, and my life is preserved.

SIT.: Jacob wrestled with God (or with an angel representing God) and prevailed. Peniel means "the face of God." USE: To show that God has a tangible form and face. *CAUTION: If it was God with whom he wrestled, it would seem to be the pre-mortal Christ. CON.: Gen. 32:24-32.*

( ) **10. Ex. 33:11**

The LORD spake unto Moses face to face, as a man speaketh unto his friend.

SIT.: Moses, while on Mt. Sinai, talked to the pre-mortal Christ and saw that he was in the form of a man. C.R.: Ex. 24:9-11; 33:21-23; Is. 6:1; Ezek. 1:26-28; 1 Ne. 2:16; Eth. 3:6-20.

See "A Testimony of The Divinity of Jesus Christ Through His Personal Manifestation," *Gifts of the Spirit,* pp. 51-68. This chapter considers many appearances of the resurrected Christ in ancient and modern times including many lesser-known appearances.

6. MEMBERS OF GODHEAD ARE
SEPARATE BEINGS

( ) **1. Acts 7:55-56**

But he, being full of the Holy Ghost, looked up
stedfastly into heaven, and saw the glory of God,
and Jesus standing on the right hand of God, And
said, Behold, I see the heavens opened, and the Son
of man standing on the right hand of God.

> *SIT.: Stephen was falsely accused and condemned
> before the Jewish Sanhedrin, before which he
> gave a great discourse. At the conclusion of this
> talk he received this important vision. CON.:
> Acts 6:5-7:60. C.R.: JS 2:17-20.*

( ) **2. Mt. 3:16-17**

Jesus, when he was baptized, went up straightway
out of the water: and, lo, the heavens were opened
unto him, and he saw the Spirit of God descending
like a dove, and lighting upon him: And lo a voice
from heaven, saying, This is my beloved Son, in
whom I am well pleased.

> *SIT.: This took place when Jesus was baptized
> by John the Baptist. CON.: Mt. 3:13-17. C.R.:
> =Mk. 1:9-11; =Lk. 3:21-22; 1 Ne. 10:9-10, 11:27.
> Also Mt. 17:5; Jn. 12:28; 3 Ne. 11:7.*

( ) **3. Heb. 1:2-3**

⌐God⌐ Hath in these last days spoken unto us by
his Son, whom he hath appointed heir of all things,

by whom also he made the worlds; Who being the brightness of his glory, and the express image of his person,...sat down on the right hand of the Majesty on high.
   C.R.: Col. 1:15-19.

( ) **4. Eph. 3:14-15**
I bow my knees unto the Father of our Lord Jesus Christ, Of whom the whole family in heaven and earth is named.
   SIT.: Paul is explaining the relationship between the members of the Godhead. CON.: Eph. 3:9-21.

( ) **5. Jn. 16:28**
I came forth from the Father, and am come into the world: again, I leave the world, and go to the Father.
   SIT.: Jesus explained his relationship to God the Father to his disciples on the Mt. of Olives shortly before his betrayal and arrest.   CON.: Jn. 16:23-29.

( ) **6. Jn. 14:28**
If ye loved me, ye would rejoice, because I said, I go unto the Father: for my Father is greater than I.
   SIT.: Jesus is talking to his disciples in the upper room following the last supper and before they go out into the Mt. of Olives. This is his discourse on the Comforter.

( ) **7. Jn. 17:20-21**
Neither pray I for these alone, but for them also

which shall believe on me through their word; That they all may be one; as thou, Father, art in me, and I in thee, that they also may be one in us: that the world may believe that thou hast sent me.

SIT.: Jesus prayed for his disciples while on the Mt. of Olives, just before his betrayal and arrest. USE: He prays that his disciples will be one like he and his father are one. Would this be in some great undiscernable mass, as other churches describe God, or one in unity and purpose? CON.: Jn. 17:1-26. C.R.: Jn. 14:20; 17:11.

( ) **8. Jn. 17:11**

Holy Father, keep through thine own name those whom thou hast given me, that they may be one, as we are.

SIT.: Jesus prayed for his disciples while on the Mt. of Olives, just before his betrayal and arrest. USE: All combined in the same being, or one in purpose? C.R.: Jn. 17:20-23; 14:20.

( ) **9. Jn. 17:5**

O Father, glorify thou me with thine own self with the glory which I had with thee before the world was.

SIT.: Christ prayed to his Father while on the Mt. of Olives, just before his betrayal and arrest.

( ) **10. Mt. 17:5**

A bright cloud overshadowed them: and behold a voice out of the cloud. which said. This is my beloved Son. in whom I am well pleased: hear ye him.

SIT.: God the Father bore witness of his Son Jesus to Peter, James, and John on the mount of transfiguration. CON.: Mt. 7:1-9. C.R.: =Mk. 9: 2-10; =Lk. 9:28-36; D & C 63:20-21. Also Mt. 3:17; Jn. 12:28; 3 Ne. 11:7.

7. RELATIONSHIP OF CHRIST
AND THE FATHER

( ) **1. 1 Cor. 8:5-6**

Though there be that are called gods, whether in heaven or in earth, (as there be gods many, and lords many,) But to us there is but one God, the Father, of whom are all things, and we in him; and one Lord Jesus Christ, by whom are all things, and we by him.

C.R.: Ps. 82:1, 6; Jn. 10:29-36.

( ) **2. Jn. 3:35**

The Father loveth the Son, and hath given all things into his hand.

SIT.: This was a portion of the testimony of John the Baptist to the divinity of Jesus. CON.: Jn. 3:25-36.

( ) **3. Jn. 13:3**

Jesus knowing that the Father had given all things into his hands, and that he was come from God, and went to God;...

SIT.: This is John's description of Jesus at the last supper.

( ) **4. Jn. 5:19**

The Son can do nothing of himself, but what he seeth the Father do: for what things soever he doeth, these also doeth the Son likewise.

SIT.: This was Jesus' sermon at the second pass-

over, in which Jesus described his relationship to his father. CON.: Jn. 5:17-47.

( ) **5. 3 Ne. 9:15**

I am Jesus Christ the Son of God. I created the heavens and the earth, and all things that in them are. I was with the Father from the beginning. I am in the Father, and the Father in me; and in me hath the Father glorified his name.

SIT.: These words were spoken from heaven following the great destruction which took place in the Americas at the time of the crucifixion of Christ.

( ) **6. Mos. 15:2-3**

Because he dwelleth in flesh he shall be called the Son of God, and having subjected the flesh to the will of the Father, being the Father and the Son— The Father, because he was conceived by the power of God; and the Son, because of the flesh; thus becoming the Father and Son.

SIT.: This was Abinadi's explanation to the wicked priests of king Noah. CON.: Mos. 15:1-9.

( ) **7. Jn. 3:16**

For God so loved the world, that he gave his only begotten Son, that whosoever believeth in him should not perish, but have everlasting life.

SIT.: Jesus said these words to Nicodemus, a ruler of the Jews who came to him by night. CON.: Jn. 3:1-21.

( ) 8. Moses 1:33

Worlds without number have I created; and I also created them for mine own purpose; and by the Son I created them, which is mine Only Begotten.

> SIT.: Moses was given this explanation of the creation when he was caught up onto an exceedingly high mountain. CON.: Moses 1:29-39.

( ) 9. Jn. 6:38

I came down from heaven, not to do mine own will, but the will of him that sent me.

> SIT.: These words were spoken by Jesus in Capernaum in his Discourse on the Bread of Life. CON.: Jn. 6:24-59.

( ) 10. Jn. 12:44-45

He that believeth on me, believeth not on me, but on him that sent me. And he that seeth me seeth him that sent me.

> SIT.: Jesus was speaking to a group of Greeks who had come to Jerusalem to celebrate the Passover. This was just following God the Father's testimony from heaven concerning the Christ. CON.: Jn: 12:20-50.

8. ROLE OF CHRIST

( ) **1. 3 Ne. 9:21**

I have come unto the world to bring redemption unto
the world, to save the world from sin.

*SIT.: These words were spoken from the heavens
following the great destruction in America at the
time of Christ's crucifixion.*

( ) **2. Jn. 14:6**

I am the way, the truth, and the life: no man cometh
unto the Father, but by me.

*SIT.: Jesus said these words to Thomas at the
last supper.*

( ) **3. Jn. 11:25-26**

I am the resurrection, and the life: he that believeth
in me, though he were dead, yet shall he live: And
whosoever liveth and believeth in me shall never die.

*SIT.: Jesus said these words to Martha as he pre-
pared to restore her brother Lazarus to life. CON.:
Jn. 11:1-45.*

( ) **4. Jn. 10:10**

I am come that they might have life, and that they
might have it more abundantly.

*SIT.: Jesus was rebuking a group of Pharisees for
their spiritual blindness. In doing so he depicted
himself as the good shepherd, and in this statement explained his mission. CON.: Jn. 9:39-10:22.*

( ) **5. Jn. 1:1-4**

In the beginning was the Word, and the Word was with
God, and the Word was God. The same was in the be-
ginning with God. All things were made by him; and
without him was not anything made that was made.
In him was life; and the life was the light of men.
SIT.: This was John's introduction to his gospel.
NOTE: The word is Christ; see Jn. 1:14. C.R.:
Col. 1:16-17; D & C 88:6-13.

( ) **6. D & C 88:6-7**

⌊Jesus Christ⌋ ascended up on high, as also he descended below all things, in that he comprehended
all things, that he might be in all and through all
things, the light of truth; Which truth shineth. This
is the light of Christ.
CON.: D & C 88:5-13. C.R.: Jn. 1:4-9; 8:12; 9:5;
D & C 84:44-46.

( ) **7. D & C 88:11-12**

The light which shineth, which giveth you light, is
through him who enlighteneth your eyes, which is
the same light that quickeneth your understandings;
Which light proceedeth forth from the presence of God
to fill the immensity of space—

( ) **8. D & C 88:13**

The light which is in all things, which giveth life to
all things, which is the law by which all things are
governed, even the power of God who sitteth upon his

throne, who is in the bosom of eternity, who is in the midst of all things.

CON.: D & C 88:6-13. C.R.: Jn. 1:4-9; 8:12; 9:5; D & C 84:44-46.

( ) 9. Jn. 6:35

I am the bread of life: he that cometh to me shall never hunger; and he that believeth on me shall never thirst.

SIT.: These words were spoken by Jesus in Capernaum in his Discourse on the Bread of Life. CON.: Jn. 6:24-59.

( ) 10. Jn. 15:13

Greater love hath no man than this, that a man lay down his life for his friends.

SIT.: These words were spoken by Jesus to his disciples shortly before he was betrayed and arrested.

9. JESUS CHRIST IS JEHOVAH

That Jesus Christ, the Lord of the New Testament, is Jehovah, the LORD of the Old Testament, is clearly seen by comparing passages from each testament in which the functions and titles of the Lord are shown. These passages are reported below in summary form and should be learned in pairs, as indicated.[1]

( ) 1. **Gen. 17:1**   The LORD said, I am the Almighty God.

       Rev. 1:8   Jesus Christ is the Almighty.

( ) 2. **Ex. 3:14-15**   The LORD is I AM.

       Jn. 8:58   While speaking of himself, Jesus said, Before Abraham was, I am.

( ) 3. **Deut. 1:32-33** The LORD led Israel out of Egypt in a cloud.

       1 Cor. 10:1-4   The cloud and spiritual rock was Christ.

( ) 4. **Ps. 96:13**   The LORD shall judge the earth.

       Jn. 5:22   The Father hath committed all judgment unto the Son.

------

[1] The word LORD (printed in small capital letters), which is frequently found in the Old Testament, represents the Hebrew word which is transliterated *Jehovah.*

( ) 5. **Is. 44:6**   The LORD said, I am the first, and I am the last.

        Rev. 1:17-18   Jesus said, I am the first and the last.

( ) 6. **Is. 45:11-12**   The LORD made the earth.

        Jn. 1:1-3, 14   All things were made by the Word, who is the only begotten Son.

( ) 7. **Is. 45:22-23**   Every knee shall bow and every tongue shall swear to the LORD.

        Phil. 2:10-11   At the name of Jesus every knee should bow and every tongue confess.

( ) 8. **Hos. 13:4**   There is no saviour beside the LORD.

        Acts 16:31   Believe on Jesus Christ, and thou shalt be saved.

( ) 9. **Zech. 14:5**   The LORD shall come with all the saints.

        1 Thess. 3:13   Jesus Christ will come with all his saints.

( ) 10. **Zech. 14:9**   The LORD shall be king over all the earth.

        Rev. 11:15   The kingdoms of this world are become the kingdoms of Christ.

37

10. KNOWLEDGE AND POWER OF GOD

( ) **1. Is. 55:8-9**

My thoughts are not your thoughts, neither are your
ways my ways, saith the LORD. For as the heavens
are higher than the earth, so are my ways higher
than your ways, and my thoughts than your thoughts.
*SIT.: These words were revealed by the Lord to
Isaiah as he defined the happy state of those who
believe in him. CON.: Is. 55:1-13.*

( ) **2. Ro. 11:33**

O the depth of the riches both of the wisdom and
knowledge of God! how unsearchable are his judgments, and his ways past finding out!
*SIT.: Paul is explaining the greatness of God.
CON.: Ro. 11:29-36. C.R.: Num. 23:19.*

( ) **3. Jas. 1:17-18**

Every good gift and every perfect gift is from above,
and cometh down from the Father of lights, with
whom is no variableness, neither shadow of turning.
Of his own will begat he us with the word of truth,
that we should be a kind of firstfruits of his crea-
tures.
*SIT.: James is showing that temptation comes
from man, not from God. CON.: Jas. 1:12-18.
C.R.: Num. 23:19.*

( ) **4. 1 Ne. 9:6**

The Lord knoweth all things from the beginning;

wherefore, he prepareth a way to accomplish all his works among the children of men; for behold, he hath all power unto the fulfilling of all his words.

SIT.: Nephi is explaining why he kept two different sets of plates. CON.: 1 Ne. 9:2-6.

( ) **5. D & C 88:41**

He comprehendeth all things, and all things are before him, and all things are round about him; and he is above all things, and in all things, and is through all things, and is round about all things; and all things are by him, and of him, even God, forever and ever.

CON.: D & C 88:40-45.

( ) **6. Jer. 32:18-19**

The Great, the Mighty God, the LORD of hosts, is his name, Great in counsel, and mighty in work: for thine eyes are open upon all the ways of the sons of men: to give every one according to his ways, and according to the fruit of his doings.

SIT.: This is a portion of a prayer offered by Jeremiah unto the Lord. CON.: Jer. 32:16-25.

( ) **7. D & C 6:16**

There is none else save God that knowest thy thoughts and the intents of thy heart.

SIT.: As a testimony to Oliver Cowdery, the Lord revealed to Joseph Smith things known only to Oliver. See D & C 6:14-24.

( ) **8. D & C 38:1-2**

Thus saith the Lord your God, even Jesus Christ, the Great I AM, Alpha and Omega, the beginning and the end, the same which looked upon the wide expanse of eternity, and all the seraphic hosts of heaven, before the world was made; The same which knoweth all things, for all things are present before mine eyes.

( ) **9. 1 Cor. 1:25**

The foolishness of God is wiser than men; and the weakness of God is stronger than men.

SIT.: Paul is explaining how God has chosen the weak things of the world to confound the things which are mighty, that no flesh should glory in his presence. CON.: 1 Cor. 1:18-31.

( ) **10. D & C 93:17**

[Jesus Christ] received all power, both in heaven and on earth; and the glory of the Father was with him, for he dwelt in him.

SIT.: In this revelation the Lord is citing the witness of John the Baptist concerning Jesus. Compare Jn. 1:19-36. CON.: D & C 93:6-18.

See ''The Nature of God and Godhood,'' *Prophets and Prophecies of The Old Testament*, pp. 76-80, for a detailed listing of passages which depict fifty-eight different attributes of God.

11. PERSONALITY OF GOD

( ) **1. D & C 20:17**

There is a God in heaven, who is infinite and eternal, from everlasting to everlasting the same unchangeable God, the framer of heaven and earth, and all things which are in them.

CON.: D & C 20:17-19.

( ) **2. Jer. 9:24**

Let him that glorieth glory in this, that he understandeth and knoweth me, that I am the LORD which exercise lovingkindness, judgment, and righteousness, in the earth: for in these things I delight, saith the LORD.

SIT.: This counsel accompanies the Lord's warning that the wise, the mighty, and the rich must not glory. CON.: Jer. 9:23-24.

( ) **3. D & C 18:10**

Remember the worth of souls is great in the sight of God.

SIT.: The Lord accompanies this admonition with an explanation of why he suffered and died for mankind. CON.: D & C 18:10-16.

( ) **4. Jn. 10:14**

I am the good shepherd, and know my sheep, and am known of mine.

SIT.: Jesus was rebuking a group of Pharisees

for their spiritual blindness. In doing so he described himself as a shepherd and his followers as sheep. *CON.: Jn. 9:39-10:22.*

( ) 5. D & C 95:1

Whom I love I also chasten that their sins may be forgiven, for with the chastisement I prepare a way for their deliverance in all things out of temptation.
  SIT.: The Lord was chastening the saints for failing to build the Kirtland Temple. CON.: D & C 95:1-6.

( ) 6. Mi. 7:18

Who is a God like unto thee, that pardoneth iniquity, and passeth by the transgression of the remnant of his heritage? he retaineth not his anger for ever, because he delighteth in mercy.
  SIT.: Micah expresses his praise for God as he grieves over the wickedness of his people.

( ) 7. Neh. 9:17

Thou art a God ready to pardon, gracious and merciful, slow to anger, and of great kindness.
  SIT.: A group of Levites gave this description of God as they reviewed the history of their people. CON.: Neh. 9:5-38.

( ) 8. Ex. 20:5-6

I the LORD thy God am a jealous God, visiting the iniquity of the fathers upon the children unto the third and fourth generation of them that hate me;

And shewing mercy unto thousands of them that love me, and keep my commandments.

SIT.: *The Lord gave this description of himself as he revealed the ten commandments unto the Israelites.* CON.: *Ex. 20:1-17.* C.R.: *Deut. 5:9-10; =Mos. 13:13-14.*

( ) **9. 2 Ne. 27:23**

I am God; and I am a God of miracles; and I will show unto the world that I am the same yesterday, today, and forever; and I work not among the children of men save it be according to their faith.

SIT.: *Nephi spoke these words of the Lord as he prophesied the coming forth of the Book of Mormon.* CON.: *2 Ne. 27:6-23.*

( ) **10. Ps. 139:7-8**

Whither shall I go from thy spirit? or whither shall I flee from thy presence? If I ascend up into heaven, thou art there: if I make my bed in hell, behold, thou art there.

SIT.: *This psalm expresses the far-reaching knowledge and influence of God. Some sects, however, attempt to use it to support the concept that God, himself, is everywhere. Note that the actual reference is to the spirit (v. 6), not to God himself.*

See ''The Nature of God and Godhood,'' *Prophets and Prophecies of The Old Testament*, pp. 76-80, for a detailed listing of passages which depict fifty-eight different attributes of God.

12. THE HOLY GHOST

( ) 1. 1 Ne. 11:11

I spake unto him as a man speaketh; for I beheld
that he was in the form of a man; yet nevertheless,
I knew that it was the Spirit of the Lord; and he
spake unto me as a man speaketh with another.

*SIT.: Nephi desired to know the interpretation of
things his father had seen. He was caught away
in the Spirit of the Lord into a high mountain.
There he conversed with the Spirit and saw that
he was in the form of a man. CON.: 1 Ne.
10:15-11:12. CAUTION: This passage is understood by some to be a reference to the pre-mortal
Christ, though such an interpretation is unlikely
in the light of 1 Ne. 10:17, 19, 22, and 11:1 and 2.
Nephi makes a special point that it is the Holy
Ghost which gives him authority to speak these
things.*

( ) 2. Jn. 14:26

The Comforter, which is the Holy Ghost, whom the
Father will send in my name, he shall teach you all
things, and bring all things to your remembrance,
whatsoever I have said unto you.

*SIT.: Jesus said these words in his Discourse
About the Comforter, which he delivered in
connection with the last supper. CON.: Jn. 14.
C.R.: Jn. 15:26; 16:13.*

( ) **3. D & C 42:17**

The Comforter knoweth all things, and beareth
record of the Father and of the Son.
CON.: D & C 42:12-17. C.R.: D & C 35:19.

( ) **4. Jn. 15:26**

When the Comforter is come, whom I will send unto
you from the Father, even the Spirit of truth, which
proceedeth from the Father, he shall testify of me.
*SIT.: Jesus said these words to his disciples af-
ter the last supper and before his arrest and betrayal. CON.: Jn. 15,16. C.R.: Jn. 14:26; 16:13.*

( ) **5. Jn. 16:13**

When he, the Spirit of truth, is come, he will guide
you into all truth: for he shall not speak of himself;
but whatsoever he shall hear, that shall he speak:
and he will shew you things to come.
*SIT.: Jesus said these words to his disciples af-
ter the last supper and before his arrest and betrayal. CON.: Jn. 15, 16. C.R.: Jn. 14:26; 15:26.*

( ) **6. D & C 68:4**

Whatsoever they shall speak when moved upon by
the Holy Ghost shall be scripture, shall be the will
of the Lord, shall be the mind of the Lord, shall be
the word of the Lord, shall be the voice of the Lord,
and the power of God unto salvation.
*SIT.: This revelation had reference to all those
who hold the priesthood. CON.: D & C 68:2-6.*

( ) **7. Mt. 12:32**

Whosoever speaketh a word against the Son of man,
it shall be forgiven him: but whosoever speaketh
against the Holy Ghost, it shall not be forgiven him,
neither in this world, neither in the world to come.

> *SIT.: Jesus was rebuking a group of Pharisees
> who was accusing him of healing by the powers
> of evil. CON.: Mt. 12:24-37. C.R.: -Mk. 3:28-29.*

( ) **8. Mt. 28:19**

Go ye therefore, and teach all nations, baptizing
them in the name of the Father, and of the Son, and
of the Holy Ghost.

> *SIT.: The resurrected Christ gave this command-
> ment to his apostles on a mountain in Galilee.
> CON.: Mt. 28:16-20. C.R.: Mk. 16:15-16.*

( ) **9. Jn. 16:8**

When he is come, he will reprove the world of sin,
and of righteousness, and of judgment.

> *SIT.: Jesus said this concerning the Holy Ghost
> as he taught his disciples following the last sup-
> per and before his betrayal and arrest. CON.:
> Jn. 15, 16.*

( ) **10. Acts 8:15-17**

[Peter and John,] when they were come down,
prayed for them, that they might receive the Holy
Ghost: (For as yet he was fallen upon none of them:
only they were baptized in the name of the Lord

Jesus.) Then laid they their hands on them, and they received the Holy Ghost.

SIT.: Philip had baptized converts in Samaria, but it was still necessary to send men with the Melchizedek Priesthood to confer the Holy Ghost upon his converts. (Philip apparently held only the lower priesthood; see Acts 6:1-6.) CON.: Acts 8:5-17.

See " A Testimony of the Divinity of Jesus Christ Through Belief in The Witness of Others," and "Godly Knowledge," *Gifts of the Spirit,* pp. 67-98, for a discussion of the Holy Ghost as a revealer of testimony and knowledge.

13. GOD ANSWERS PRAYERS

1. 1 Kings 3:5-15   (Story)   Solomon's Prayer

A. The Lord appeared to Solomon in a dream, and said to him, "Ask what I shall give thee."

B. Solomon asked the Lord for an understanding heart to judge the people.

C. The Lord was pleased that he had not asked for a long life, for riches, or for the death of his enemies. He said, "Behold, I have done according to thy words: lo, I have given thee a wise and an understanding heart."

D. Then the Lord also promised him riches and honor, and told him that if he would keep the commandments the Lord would also lengthen his days.

> *SIT.: This blessing was given to Solomon shortly after he was anointed king. As examples of the great wisdom he received see his judgment between the two mothers (1 Ki. 3:16-28) and his many wise sayings (the book of Proverbs; 1 Ki. 4:29-34).*

2. James 1:5

If any of you lack wisdom, let him ask of God, that giveth to all men liberally, and upbraideth not; and it shall be given him.

SIT.: This advice was written by James in his general epistle. It was this passage which caused Joseph Smith to seek and receive his first vision (see JS 2:11).

3. Joseph Smith 2:5-20 (Story) Joseph Smith's First Vision

A. There was great excitement among the churches in upper New York where Joseph Smith lived. All the churches were trying to win new converts.

B. Joseph wanted to join a church but didn't know which was God's true church.

C. One day he was reading in the Bible and read James 1:5, which says, " If any of you lack wisdom, let him ask of God, that giveth to all men liberally, and upbraideth not; and it shall be given him.''

D. Joseph believed the promise he read, and he decided to go to a place where he would be alone and pray for an answer to his question.

E. One morning in the early spring of 1820, Joseph went into the woods near his home to pray.

F. As he began to pray, an evil power seized him. He was surrounded by darkness and was almost unable to pray. The power almost destroyed Joseph, but he called upon God to save him.

G. Suddenly a light appeared above him which drove the evil force away. He saw two persons surrounded with light and glory. One called Joseph by name and said, "This is my Beloved Son. Hear him!"

H.   Joseph asked which of the churches he should join. He was told to join none of them, for they were all wrong.

I.   Joseph was also told that
1. the creeds of the churches were an abomination
2. the people of the churches talked about Jesus but their hearts were far from him
3. their doctrines were the commands of men
4. they denied the power of God.

J.   From his first vision Joseph learned that
1. God the Father and Jesus Christ are separate, real persons
2. God hears and answers prayers
3. God's church was not then on the earth.
   SIT.: Joseph Smith 2 is the prophet's account of the restoration of the gospel which he published in 1842. C.R.: (God the Father speaks from the heavens) Mt. 3:17; 17:5; Jn. 12:28; 3 Ne. 11:7. (The words of Christ prophesied) Is. 29:13; but also Mt. 15:7-9.

4. Doctrine and Covenants 88:63

Draw near unto me and I will draw near unto you;

seek me diligently and ye shall find me; ask, and ye shall receive; knock, and it shall be opened unto you.

SIT.: This revelation was given to the church through Joseph Smith in 1832.

14. GOD BLESSES THOSE WHO HAVE FAITH

1. **1 Samuel 17**   (Story)   **David Slays Goliath**

   A.   The Philistines had attacked Israel. Saul, the king of Israel, gathered his army to fight against them.

   B.   The Philistines had a giant ten feet high named Goliath who challenged the Israelites to send out a man to fight him. The Israelites were afraid and no one was willing to go and fight him.

   C.   David, a young shepherd boy, had his three oldest brothers in Saul's army. David was sent by his father to take food to his brothers while the armies were lined up against each other.

   D.   David came to the battlefield and heard Goliath's boasts. He asked, "Who is this uncircumcised Philistine, that he should defy the armies of the living God?" David was taken to King Saul and he volunteered to fight Goliath.

   E.   David told Saul how the Lord had helped him when his flocks had been attacked by a lion and by a bear, and said that God would help him kill Goliath too. Saul agreed to let David fight the giant.

   F.   Saul put his armor on David, but David had it taken off because it was too big for him. Then he went and chose five smooth stones and put them in his shepherd's bag. He went to fight Goliath with his staff and his sling.

G. Goliath made fun of David, but David told him, "I come to thee in the name of the Lord of Hosts, the God of the armies of Israel, whom thou hast defied. This day will the Lord deliver thee into mine hand."

H. Goliath came to attack David, but David put a stone in his sling, threw it, and hit Goliath in the forehead. Goliath fell to the earth. David ran and took Goliath's sword and cut off the giant's head.

I. When they saw that Goliath had been killed the Israelites took courage, attacked, and defeated the army of the Philistines.

SIT.: Though the people of Israel did not know it, David had already been anointed to be the next king of Israel by the prophet Samuel (1 Sam. 16:13) and " the Spirit of the Lord came upon David from that day forward."

2. **Matthew 14:22-33 (Story) Peter Walks On The Water**

A. Jesus crossed the Sea of Galilee with his disciples. He left them in the boat while he went to pray.

B. The wind moved the boat away from the shore into the middle of the sea.

C. Jesus returned to the boat by walking on the water. When the disciples saw him coming they were frightened and thought that they were seeing a spirit. Jesus called to them and told them, "It is I; be not afraid."

D. Peter called out, "Lord, if it be thou, bid me come unto thee on the water." The Lord told Peter to come.

E. Peter climbed out of the boat and began to walk on the top of the water. Then he realized how rough the sea was and became afraid. When fear entered him he began to sink. He cried to the Lord to save him.

F. Jesus reached out and caught him, and said to him, "O thou of little faith, wherefore didst thou doubt?"

G. When they were back in the ship the wind stopped. The disciples came and worshipped Jesus.

> *SIT.: Peter should have had greater faith, for earlier that day the apostles had seen Jesus miraculously provide food for five thousand men and their women and children. The accounts in Mark and John do not mention Peter's role in the affair. C.R.: ▪Mk. 6:45-52; ▪Jn. 6:15-21.*

3. Matthew 8:5-13 (Story) Jesus Heals The Centurion's Servant

A. A Roman officer came to Jesus at Capernaum and told the Lord that his servant was very sick. Jesus said he would come and heal him.

B. The officer said he was not worthy for the Lord to come into his home, but said that if Jesus would speak the word he knew his servant would be healed, just as the officer could command his men and have them obey him.

C. Jesus marvelled at his faith and said, "I have not found so great faith, no, not in Israel."

D. Jesus told the officer, "Go thy way, and as thou hast believed, so be it done unto thee."

E. The Centurion's servant was healed the same hour.

> *SIT.: This miracle took place just after Jesus had taught his* Sermon on the Mount. *The following day he raised the son of the widow of Nain from the dead. C.R.: =Lk. 7:1-10.*

4. Mark 5:24-34 (Story) Jesus Heals the Woman Who Touches His Hem

A. Jesus was walking through a large crowd. Many people were bumping against him.

B. A woman came up behind him and touched his clothes. This woman had suffered with an issue of blood for twelve years and no doctor had been able to heal it. She believed that if she could touch Jesus she would be healed.

C.   She touched the hem of Jesus' garment and was healed. Jesus felt virtue go out of him. He asked, "Who touched my clothes?"

D.   The woman felt that she was healed but was very frightened. She fell down before Jesus and told him her story.

E.   Jesus said, "Daughter, thy faith hath made thee whole; go in peace, and be whole of thy plague."

> *SIT.: The location of this miracle is uncertain. It took place shortly after Jesus had cast out evil spirits from the man of Gadarene and the evil spirits had entered a herd of swine and had run into the sea. When this healing took place Jesus was on his way to raise the daughter of Jairus from the dead. C.R.: =Lk. 8:43-48; =Mt. 9:20-22; 14:36.*

5. 1 Samuel 1   (Story)   The Birth of Samuel

A.   Hannah, the wife of Elkanah, had been unable to have children. This made her sad and bitter.

B.   One day when she came to the temple she made a vow to the Lord. She promised the Lord that if he would give her a son, she would give him to the Lord to serve him all his life.

C.   Eli the priest saw her praying and spoke to her. When he heard what Hannah had told the Lord he told her, "Go in peace: and the

God of Israel grant thee thy petition that thou hast asked of him.''

D. The Lord remembered her and gave her a son. She called him Samuel.

E. When Samuel was old enough to leave his mother, Hannah took him to Eli at the temple and had Eli raise him in the service of the Lord.

SIT.: See Hannah's beautiful prayer of praise: 1 Sam. 2:1-10.

15. GOD PROTECTS AND BLESSES THOSE WHO SERVE HIM

1. **Exodus 16:1-31** (Story) **The Lord Provides the Israelites With Manna and Quail**

A. The children of Israel had wandered in the wilderness for about six weeks since they left Egypt. Their food was gone, and they were afraid they would starve in the desert.

B. The Lord spoke to his prophet, Moses, and promised that he would send them bread from heaven.

C. That evening a flock of quails came and landed in the camp, which provided them with meat. The next morning the people found small bits of food which they were able to gather and eat.

D. Moses told the people to use the manna up each day. Those who kept it over till the next morning found that it went bad.

E. Moses told the people to gather a double portion on the night before the sabbath and then not to gather any on the sabbath day. This manna didn't go bad when kept over night. Num. 11:6-9.

   SIT.: Manna described: Ex. 16:14-15; The Lord provided manna for the Israelites for forty years, until they entered into Canaan (Josh. 5:11-12).

2. **1 Kings 17:1-7** (Story) **The Lord Sends Ravens to Feed Elijah**

    A.   The King of Israel, Ahab, was very wicked. He had made his people worship idols and false gods.

    B.   The Lord's prophet, Elijah punished Ahab by withholding the dew and the rain.

    C.   The Lord commanded Elijah to hide from Ahab by the brook Cherith, near the Jordan River.

    D.   Elijah stayed by the brook where water was available. The Lord sent ravens with bread and meat to Elijah each morning and evening.
        SIT.: Other prophets have also been able to withhold the rains and bring famines. See Hel. 11:1-17; Eth. 9:28-35; Rev. 11: 3-6. C.R.: Jas. 5:16-18.

3. **1 Kings 17:8-24** (Story) **Elijah Blesses the Widow of Zaraphath**

    A.   The Lord commanded Elijah to leave the brook Cherith and to travel to Zaraphath, where a widow was to sustain him during the time of famine.

    B.   When Elijah came to Zaraphath he found the widow and asked her for food and water.

    C.   She said that she only had a bit of meal in a barrel and a few drops of oil. She was about to eat one last meal with her son and thought that she then would soon die.

    D.   Elijah told her that if she would prepare

some food for him the barrel of meal and jar
of oil would not be empty until rain fell a-
gain on the earth.

E.   She did as Elijah said, and there was food
for the three of them for many days, for
her barrel and jar did not become empty.

F.   The widow's son grew sick and died.

G.   Elijah carried the boy's body to a bed,
where he prayed that the Lord would restore his life.

H.   The boy's spirit returned to his body and he
was returned to life.

I.   The woman said, "Now by this I know that
thou art a man of God, and that the word of
the Lord in thy mouth is truth."

*SIT.: Elijah's disciple, Elisha, also
brought a boy back to life. See 2 Ki.
4:18-37.*

4. Daniel 3:1-30   (Story)   Three Israelites Are Saved From the Fiery Furnace

A.   Nebuchadnezzar, the king of Babylon, made
a golden image ninety feet high. He commanded all the officials of his kingdom to
come to the dedication of the image.

B.   When the dedication began, it was commanded that when the trumpet blew, everyone was
to fall down and worship the image. If they
didn't, they would be thrown into a fiery
furnace.

C.   Shadrach, Meshach, and Abednego, three
men who worshipped Jehovah, refused to
worship the idol.

D.   Nebuchadnezzar called them before him to

question them. They said that they did not know if their God would save them from the fiery furnace, but that they would not worship false gods.

E. Nebuchadnezzar became angry and had the furnace heated seven times hotter than normal. The three men were bound and tossed into the furnace. The heat was so hot that it killed the men who threw them in.

F. God sent an angel who untied them and walked with them in the fiery furnace. The heat did not harm them.

G. Nebuchadnezzar called them out of the furnace. He made a decree that anyone who spoke against their God should be killed, saying that "there is no other God that can deliver after this sort."

H. Nebuchadnezzar promoted Shadrach, Meshach, and Abednego in his kingdom.

SIT.: This took place in Babylon after Babylonia had conquered Judah. The three Israelites were children of Jewish nobility who were taken into captivity in the first deportation. See Dan. 1:1-7.

5. Matthew 20:1-16   Christ's Parable of the Laborers in the Vineyard

A. Jesus told the story of a householder who went to hire laborers in his vineyard.

B. The householder found a group of men about six a.m. and agreed to pay them a penny to work the day in his vineyard. They went to work.

C. About nine a.m. the householder sent an-

61

other group to work, telling them he would pay them a fair wage.

D. About noon he sent another group to work, and three hours after that he sent still another group to work. He told them all that he would pay them a fair wage.

E. Shortly before sundown he found still others whom he sent to work, telling them that he would pay them a fair wage.

F. At the end of the day the householder paid them all. He gave every man a penny, which was a fair wage for a full day's work.

G. Those who worked the full day complained, saying that they should be paid more than those who worked only a short time.

H. The householder told them that he had paid them what he agreed, and said that those who had worked all day long had been treated fairly.

SIT.: Jesus was preaching in Judea beyond the Jordan River. His disciples had inquired about their rewards in the future life, and Jesus was explaining the principle that the first shall be last and the last shall be first. MEANING: The householder = the Lord. The day = man's mortal life. The wage = entry into the Lord's kingdom. Even those who hear and accept the gospel and aren't able to begin to labor for the Lord until late in their life can gain the full blessings of his kingdom.

6. Acts 12:1-19 (Story) Peter Is Delivered From Prison

A. King Herod began to persecute the leaders of the church.

B. He captured the apostle Peter and held him in prison.

C. Peter was sleeping chained to two soldiers. Other soldiers guarded the doors of the prison.

D. An angel woke Peter. The chains fell from off his hands.

E. Peter followed the angel through the prison, past the gate, to freedom. He went to where a group of church members were gathered.

F. The soldiers at the prison didn't even know what had happened to Peter.

> *SIT.: The Herod who was persecuting Peter was Herod Agrippa I. He died shortly after Peter escaped. Other miraculous escapes of the Lord's servants are recorded in the scriptures. See Al. 14:3-28; Hel. 5:20-52; Acts 16:23-34.*

7. Acts 27, 28:1-10 (Story) Paul Is Saved From a Shipwreck

A. Paul was a prisoner of the Romans and was being taken to Rome in a ship to stand trial.

B. By the time they reached the island of Crete it was late in the season and winter was approaching. Paul advised them to stay there for the winter but they sailed on against his counsel.

C. A terrible storm came up and they feared

that everyone would be lost.

D.　Paul fasted, and an angel appeared to him and told him that he must be brought before Ceasar and that no lives would be lost.

E.　The crew tried to dock the ship on the island of Melita but it ran aground and broke up. The people all swam to shore safely.

F.　They made a fire. As Paul gathered some sticks, a snake bit his hand. The people expected him to die but he was not harmed.

G.　Paul was also able to administer to many who were sick and heal them.

SIT.: Melita is a small island about seventy miles southwest of Sicily. God's servants are promised protection from the bites of serpents: see D & C 84:65-73; Mk. 16:17-18.

8. 1 Nephi 3, 4　(Story)　Nephi Obtains the Brass Plates of Laban

A.　The prophet Lehi and his family had obeyed the Lord's commandment to flee out of Jerusalem into the wilderness.

B.　Lehi sent his sons back to Jerusalem to obtain the scriptures which were written on plates of brass.

C.　Nephi went back with his brothers Sam, Laman and Lemuel to obtain the brass plates.

D.　The brothers drew lots to decide who should go and talk to Laban, who had the plates in his possession. Laman was chosen. When Laman tried to talk to Laban, Laban accused Laman of being a thief and drove him away.

E.   The four brothers went and obtained the gold and silver they had left behind in Jerusalem and tried to buy the plates from Laban, but Laban took their money and then sent his servants to kill them. The brothers fled into the wilderness.

F.   Laman and Lemuel became angry with their younger brothers and began to beat them. An angel appeared and stopped them. The angel commanded them to go back to Jerusalem and said that the Lord would deliver Laban into their hands.

G.   Nephi went into Jerusalem by night, and was led by the Holy Spirit. He found Laban lying drunk in the street.

H.   The Holy Ghost commanded Nephi to take Laban's sword and kill him. Nephi didn't want to kill him but the Spirit said that "it is better that one man should perish than that a nation should dwindle and perish in unbelief."

I.   Nephi obeyed the Spirit and slew Laban. He then put on Laban's clothes and went to Laban's treasury and commanded the servant to get the brass plates and follow him. The servant thought that Nephi was Laban and did as he was told.

J.   When they were beyond the walls of Jerusalem, Nephi seized the servant and told him his life would be spared if he would come with them into the wilderness. The servant, Zoram, swore that he would follow them and they took the plates back to Lehi.
     NOTE: The Bible records many instances

*where the Lord's servants destroy the
wicked as Nephi did Laban. See Josh.
6:17-21; 7:10-26; 8:25-27; 10:40-42; 1 Sam.
15:1-26; 1 Ki. 18:20-40; 2 Ki. 1:9-15.*

9. 1 Nephi 18   (Story)   Nephi Is Protected From His Wicked Brothers

A.   Nephi and his brothers built a ship and set
sail for the promised land.

B.   After they had sailed for many days Laman
and Lemuel forgot that the Lord had been
guiding them and began to dance and sing
and to act with great rudeness.

C.   Nephi tried to correct them but they rejected
his words and tied him up.

D.   When they tied up Nephi the Lord made
their compass, the Liahona, stop working.

E.   A terrible storm arose and drove their boat
back for three days. On the fourth day it became so bad that Laman and Lemuel could
see that the judgments of God were upon
them. They untied Nephi.

F.   Through his faith and prayers Nephi was
able to make the storm cease and the compass begin to work again.

*NOTE: For other instances in which Ne-
phi was miraculously protected from his
evil brothers see 1 Ne. 3:28-30; 7:16-21;
17:48-55; 2 Ne. 5:1-6.*

10. Alma 17:19-18:40   (Story)   Ammon Defends the Flocks of King Lamoni

A.   Ammon went to do missionary work among

the Lamanites.

B. When he entered their land, the Lamanites seized him and brought him before King Lamoni.

C. Ammon told the king he wished to live a-mong the Lamanites. This pleased the king so much that he offered to let Ammon marry one of his daughters. Ammon refused but said he would like to be one of the king's servants.

D. Ammon went with the king's servants to tend his flocks near the waters of Sebus. A group of Lamanite robbers came and scattered the flocks. The king's servants were afraid that the king would put them to death for not protecting the flocks.

E. Ammon got the other servants to go and re-gather the flocks. The robbers attacked a-gain. Ammon fought with the robbers while the other servants guarded the flocks.

F. The Lord blessed Ammon and protected him so that the robbers could not hit him with their slings and stones. Ammon killed so many robbers with his sling that the other robbers were astonished.

G. The robbers came closer and attacked Am-mon with clubs. When they attacked Ammon was able to cut off their arms with his sword before they hit him. He killed the robber leader and drove the rest away.

H. The other servants went and told King La-moni what Ammon had done. Instead of seek-ing the king's praise, Ammon went and took care of the king's horses.

I. When Ammon was called before the king, he

was able to know the king's thoughts by the power of the Holy Ghost.

J.   Ammon was able to preach the gospel to the king, and King Lamoni believed his words because he knew that God was with Ammon.
SIT.: Ammon was a son of King Mosiah (Mos. 27:34) and was chief among his brothers who were missionaries (Al. 17: 11-18). For the account of King Lamoni's conversion see Al. 18:40-19:36.

11. Alma 56   (Story)   The Two Thousand Sons of Helaman

A.   A group of Lamanites were converted to the gospel. They took an oath never to shed blood any more, and came to live among the Nephites. Later there was another war between the Nephites and the Lamanites.

B.   The group of converted Lamanites wanted to help the Nephites defend their country. The prophet Helaman reminded them about their oath and told them not to fight.

C.   The converted Lamanites had many young sons who had not taken the oath. They decided to let 2,000 of their sons go and fight, with Helaman as their leader. Helaman led his army to help Antipus, a Nephite general.

D.   The 2,000 young warriors "had been taught by their mothers, that if they did not doubt, God would deliver them."

E.   A fierce battle was fought in which many died on both sides, but the young warriors were given miraculous strength and not one of them was killed.

> *SIT.: The converted Lamanites were called Anti-Nephi-Lehies. They were converts of the sons of Mosiah (Al. 23). Their covenant is recorded in Al. 24. The sons of Helaman were preserved in other battles also: see Al. 57:24-27. C.R.:Al. 58:10-11; 40.*

12. Helaman 5 (Story) Nephi and Lehi Are Protected by Fire

A. Nephi and Lehi, the sons of Helaman, went to do missionary work among the Lamanites.

B. An army of Lamanites captured them and put them in prison, where they were left for many days without food.

C. About three hundred of the Lamanites came into the prison to slay them. Suddenly Nephi and Lehi were surrounded by fire. The fire didn't burn them, but it kept the Lamanites from harming them.

D. The earth began to tremble and a cloud of darkness came into the prison so that the Lamanites could not see. From above the cloud a voice spoke three times telling them to repent and stop trying to harm God's servants.

E. Aminadab, one of the men in the prison, suddenly saw the faces of Nephi and Lehi through the darkness. He called the others and they could all see the two missionaries.

F. When the Lamanites asked Aminadab what they should do, he told them they must all repent and cry unto God until they had faith. They began to do this and the darkness disappeared and they were all surrounded by pillars of fire.

G. The Holy Ghost came and entered into them and angels ministered unto them. The three hundred Lamanites went out and told what had happened to them throughout the area. Many were converted.

> *NOTE: For other examples of the Holy Ghost being manifested through a visible fire see Acts 2:1-4, 3 Ne. 17:24, and* History of the Church *2:386, 428.*

16. THE LORD IS A GOD OF MIRACLES AND POWER

1. John 20:31

These [miracles] are written, that ye might believe that Jesus is the Christ, the Son of God; and that believing ye might have life through his name.

SIT.: The context shows that John had specific reference to the events following the resurrection of Christ, yet is equally applicable to all of the Savior's miracles.

2. John 2:1-11 (Story) Jesus Turns Water into Wine

A. Jesus attended a wedding feast in Cana with his mother and some of his disciples.

B. During the feast the host ran out of wine.

C. Jesus' mother asked him to provide more wine.

D. Jesus had the servants fill six waterpots with water.

E. When they served it to the ruler of the feast, he found it was turned into wine. He thought it was the best wine served during the feast.

SIT : Although this is the first miracle performed by Jesus to be recorded in the Bible. it undoubtedly was not the first miracle he had performed. His mother certainly would not have insisted that Jesus work a miracle in front of other

*people unless she had seen his power
manifested previously.*

3. **Mark 4:36-41** **(Story)** **Jesus Calms the
Storm**

    A.   Jesus sailed with his disciples across the
Sea of Galilee.

    B.   While Jesus was asleep in the rear of the
boat, a great storm arose and the boat began
to fill with water.

    C.   His disciples awoke Jesus, saying, "Master,
carest thou not that we perish?"

    D.   Jesus arose, rebuked the wind, and told the
sea, "Peace, be still."

    E.   The wind stopped blowing and there was a
great calm.

    F.   The disciples were amazed and frightened,
and said, "What manner of man is this, that
even the wind and the sea obey him?"

        C.R.: =Lk. 8:22-25; =Mt. 8:23-27.

4. **Mark 6:33-44** **(Story)** **Jesus Feeds the Five
Thousand**

    A.   A large group of people gathered to hear
Jesus preach.

    B.   At the end of the day, the apostles wanted
to send the crowd away, but Jesus told them
to give the people something to eat.

    C.   The apostles checked and found they only
had five loaves and two fishes.

D. Jesus had the people sit down in groups of hundreds and groups of fifties. Then he blessed the food and divided it up.

E. The apostles were able to serve the entire group until they were all filled, and then gathered up twelve baskets of leftover food.

F. The Lord had provided food for five thousand men plus their women and children.
    C.R.: =Mt. 14:14-21; =Lk. 9:11-17; =Jn. 6:1-14. See also Jesus' feeding of the four thousand: Mt. 15:29-38; Mk. 8:1-9.

5. Matthew 17:14-21   (Story)   Jesus Casts Out an Evil Spirit

A. A man came to Jesus and asked the Master to heal his son, for he was possessed by an evil spirit and often fell into the fire or into the water.

B. The man said that his disciples had tried to heal the child and had been unable to do so.

C. Jesus rebuked the devil and the evil spirit went out of the child, leaving him healed.

D. The disciples later came to Jesus and asked why they had been unable to cast the evil spirit out.

E. Jesus said they couldn't cast the evil spirit out because of their unbelief. He told them, "If ye have faith...nothing shall be impossible to you."

F. Jesus also explained that this type of evil

spirit could only be cast out by the disciples through prayer and fasting.

SIT.: This occurred just after Jesus had gone to the mount of transfiguration with Peter, James and John and they had been visited by Moses and Elias. C.R.: =Mk. 9:14-29; =Lk. 9:37-43. For other instances of evil spirits being cast out see Mk. 1:21-28; Lk. 8:26-39; Mt. 9:32-34; Lk. 11:14-26.

6. **John 11:1-45   (Story)   Jesus Raises Lazarus from the Dead**

A. A man from Bethany named Lazarus became sick.

B. His sisters, Mary and Martha, sent to Jesus and asked him to come and heal Lazarus.

C. Jesus said, "This sickness is not unto death, but for the glory of God." He waited two days before traveling to Bethany.

D. When Jesus and his disciples came to Bethany, they found that Lazarus had been dead for four days and was buried in a tomb.

E. Martha and Mary met Jesus and said that if he had been there, their brother would not have died.

F. Jesus went to the tomb and had the stone removed from the door.

G. Jesus prayed to his Father and then called out, "Lazarus, come forth."

H. Lazarus rose from the dead and walked from the tomb.

> *NOTE: Jesus raised others from the dead;
> see Lk. 7:12-17; 8:41-42, 49-55. The
> Bible also tells of others being restored
> to life: Acts 9:36-42; 20:6-12; 1 Ki.
> 17:17-24; 2 Ki. 4:18-37.*

**7.   Luke 17:11-19   (Story)   Jesus Heals Ten
Lepers**

A.   Jesus passed through Galilee and Samaria
on his way to Jerusalem.

B.   As he entered a village, ten men with
leprosy called to him, saying, "Master,
have mercy on us."

C.   Jesus told them to go and show themselves
to the priest.

D.   As the ten went to the priest, they found
that they were healed from their leprosy.

E.   One of the ten returned to Jesus, glorified
God, and thanked him.

F.   Jesus asked where the other nine were, and
then told the thankful man, "Thy faith hath
made thee whole."

> *NOTE: The laws concerning leprosy are
> found in Lev. 13, 14.*

17. GOD PUNISHES THE WICKED

1. **Genesis 6, 7**   (Story)   **Noah and the Flood**

   A. God saw that the wickedness of men was great on the earth, and that the people of the earth thought about evil things continually. The earth was corrupt and filled with violence.

   B. The only righteous men on earth were Noah and his sons. The Lord told Noah to build a huge ark. He told Noah he was going to destroy every living thing on the earth except his family and the animals he took into the ark.

   C. The ark was to be 450 feet long. 75 feet wide. and 45 feet high. It was to have three different stories. The ark took 120 years to build.

   D. When Noah was six hundred years old the flood came upon the earth. He and his wife, his three sons and their wives. all went into the ark. They took seven pairs of each of the clean beasts and two of all other animals.

   E. The water covered the earth for a hundred and fifty days. and every man was killed except those on the ark.

   NOTE God established the rainbow as a sign that he would never again destroy the earth by flood: Gen. 9:11-17. C R. Heb. 11:7: 2 Pet. 2:5.

2. **Genesis 18:17-19:26** (Story) **Sodom and Gomorrah Are Destroyed**

A. The Lord told Abraham that he was displeased with the wickedness of the people of Sodom and Gomorrah.

B. Abraham asked the Lord if he would destroy the righteous with the wicked. He asked if the city could be spared if there were fifty righteous people in it. The Lord said that he would spare it if there were that many good people there.

C. Abraham asked what the Lord would do if there were only forty-five, or forty, or thirty, or twenty, or ten who were righteous there. Each time the Lord said he would spare the city if there were only that many who were righteous. Then the Lord went away.

D. Abraham's nephew, Lot, lived in Sodom. Two angels came to visit him. Evil men of Sodom surrounded his house and tried to capture the angels. The angels finally blinded the evil men who tried to capture them.

E. The angels told Lot to flee out of the city with his wife and two daughters, because the city was about to be destroyed. They were commanded not to look back. Lot's wife looked back and was turned into a pillar of salt.

F. The Lord rained fire and brimstone on

Sodom and Gomorrah and the cities were destroyed.

C.R.: 2 Pet. 2:6-9; Lk. 17:26-32.

3. **Numbers 16:1-33** **(Story)** **The Rebellion of Korah**

A. Korah and his followers challenged Moses' authority to lead the Israelites.

B. Moses told Korah that tomorrow the Lord would show the people whether he wanted Korah or Moses to be his prophet.

C. The next day Korah and all his followers gathered at the door of their tabernacle.

D. The glory of the Lord appeared to all the congregation, and the Lord told Moses to have all the righteous people stand back from Korah's followers so that he could destroy the wicked ones. The people stood back.

E. Then Moses gave the people a sign. He said that if the Lord opened the earth and swallowed up Korah and his followers, then the people would know that they had provoked the Lord.

F. Then the earth opened up and swallowed Korah and his followers and all their houses and belongings. In this way the Lord taught his people not to rebel against their prophet.

SIT.: This rebellion took place at Kadesh-Barnea about fifteen months after the Israelites had left the land of Egypt.

78

4. **2 Kings 5** (Story) **Gehazi Is Smitten with Leprosy**

   A. A Syrian army officer had leprosy. One of his wife's servants told him that Elisha the prophet could heal him.

   B. Naaman came to visit Elisha. The prophet sent word that he should go and wash in the river Jordan seven times and he would be healed.

   C. Naaman washed himself in the Jordan River and was healed. He came back to Elisha and wanted to give the prophet a gift. Elisha refused and would not accept it.

   D. Elisha's servant, Gehazi, decided to try to get some of the reward Naaman had offered to the prophet. He ran after Naaman and told him that Elisha had changed his mind and would accept a reward. Silver and clothing were given to him.

   E. Elisha asked Gehazi where he had been. Gehazi lied and said that he had not gone out. Elisha knew what Gehazi had done and punished him by cursing him with Naaman's leprosy.

   F. Leprosy immediately came upon Gehazi. *NOTE: Other prophets have been able to smite people with diseases; see 1 Ki. 13:4-6; 2 Chron. 21:12-20.*

5. **1 Samuel 15** (Story) **Saul is Rejected as King**

   A. The prophet Samuel came to Saul, the king

79

of Israel, and told him that he was commanded of the Lord to fight against the Amalekites. Because they were so evil, Saul was to kill every person and animal.

B. Saul fought the battle and won, but decided to spare Agag, the king of the Amalekites. He also spared the best of their animals to use for burnt offerings. When he spared them he disobeyed the Lord.

C. The Lord spoke to the prophet Samuel and told him he had rejected Saul as king because of his disobedience.

D. Samuel came to Saul and gave him the Lord's message. When Saul said he had saved the animals to offer as sacrifices, Samuel told him, "To obey is better than sacrifice, and to hearken than the fat of rams."

E. The prophet Samuel took the wicked king Agag and killed him.

F. Samuel left and never came to see Saul again.

NOTE: The scriptures record many instances where the Lord's servants destroy the wicked as Samuel did Agag. See 1 Ne. 3, 4; Josh. 6:17-21; 7:10-26; 8:25-27; 10:40-42; 1 Ki. 18:20-40; 2 Ki. 1:9-15; Ex. 32.

6. **Acts 5** (Story) **Ananias and Sapphira Try to Rob the Lord**

A. Ananias and his wife, Sapphira, sold some

property. They had agreed to donate all they earned from the sale to the Lord. They decided to hold back part of the money and not give it all to the Lord.

B. When Ananias brought part of the money to the apostle Peter, the apostle said, "Ananias, why hath Satan filled thine heart to lie to the Holy Ghost, and to keep back part of the price of the land?"

C. Because of his wickedness, Ananias suddenly fell dead. He was taken out and buried.

D. Three hours later Sapphira came in, looking for her husband. Peter asked her how much they had sold the land for. She lied and told Peter the false figure upon which she and her husband had agreed.

E. Peter challenged her, saying, "How is it that ye have agreed together to tempt the Spirit of the Lord?" He told her that her husband had died.

F. Because of her wickedness, Sapphira suddenly fell dead also. They carried her out and buried her.

SIT.: At this time the Saints were living under a form of the United Order, in which they had pooled their goods and had all things in common. See Acts 4:32-37; 2:44-46; 6:1-3.

18. APOSTASY PREDICTED

( ) 1. 2 Thess. 2:3-4

Let no man deceive you by any means: for that day
shall not come, except there come a falling away
first, and that man of sin be revealed, the son of perdition; Who opposeth and exalteth himself above all
that is called God, or that is worshipped; so that he
as God sitteth in the temple of God, shewing himself that he is God.

*SIT.: The Saints at Thessalonica had come to be-
lieve that the second coming of Christ was im-
inent. Paul wrote to them and told them that that
day (of Christ's coming) would not arrive until
after an apostasy had taken place. CON.: 2 Thess.
2:1-12.*

( ) 2. Rev. 13:7-8

It was given unto him to make war with the saints,
and to overcome them: and power was given him over
all kindreds, and tongues, and nations. And all that
dwell upon the earth shall worship him, whose names
are not written in the book of life of the Lamb.

*SIT.: John the Revelator prophesied of an enemy
of the saints which he depicted as a beast. Although interpretations may vary as to the exact
nature of the beast, yet it is obvious that he was
evil, would war against the saints, and would
gain the advantage until all the people of the
earth would worship him. CON.: Rev. 13:1-10.*

( ) 3. Is. 29:9-10

Stay yourselves, and wonder; cry ye out, and cry:

they are drunken, but not with wine; they stagger, but not with strong drink. For the LORD hath poured out upon you the spirit of deep sleep, and hath closed your eyes: the prophets and your rulers, the seers hath he covered.

SIT.: This prophecy of the apostasy is linked with other prophecies pertaining to the restoration and the Book of Mormon (see 3-5). The verses which follow indicate that it will be the Book of Mormon (the book that is sealed) which will be "the vision of all." CON.: Is. 29:1-14.

( ) **4. Lk. 11:49-50**

Therefore also said the wisdom of God, I will send them prophets and apostles, and some of them they shall slay and persecute: That the blood of all the prophets, which was shed from the foundation of the world, may be required of this generation.

SIT.: Jesus rebuked the Pharisees and lawyers as he sat at dinner with them. CON.: Lk. 11:37-54. USE: This passage provides an answer for the often-asked question, why would Christ allow the church he had established to be taken from the earth?

( ) **5. 2 Tim. 3:1-2, 5**

This know also, that in the last days perilous times shall come. For men shall be lovers of their own selves, covetous, boasters, proud, blasphemers, disobedient to parents, unthankful, unholy,...Having a form of godliness, but denying the power thereof: from such turn away.

CON.: 2 Tim. 3:1-13. C.R.: Is. 29:13; J.S. 2:19.

( ) **6. 1 Tim. 4:1-3**

Now the Spirit speaketh expressly, that in the latter times some shall depart from the faith, giving heed to seducing spirits, and doctrines of devils; Speaking lies in hypocrisy; having their conscience seared with a hot iron; Forbidding to marry, and commanding to abstain from meats.

C.R.: D & C 49:15-21.

( ) **7. Mt. 24:24**

There shall arise false Christs, and false prophets, and shall shew great signs and wonders; insomuch that, if it were possible, they shall deceive the very elect.

SIT.: This prophecy was made by Jesus to his disciples in his great discourse on the last days which he made on the Mt. of Olives three days before his death. CON.: Mt. 24:3-51. C R.: Mk. 13: 1-37; Lk. 21:5-36. CAUTION: The context of this passage shows that its fulfillment is yet future.

( ) **8. Is. 24:5-6**

The earth also is defiled under the inhabitants thereof; because they have transgressed the laws, changed the ordinance, broken the everlasting covenant. Therefore hath the curse devoured the earth, and they that dwell therein are desolate; therefore the inhabitants of the earth are burned, and few men left.

CON.: Is. 24:1-12. CAUTION: While this prophecy speaks of an apostasy, its fulfillment is yet future.

( ) **9. Acts 20:29-30**

I know this, that after my departing shall grievous wolves enter in among you, not sparing the flock. Also of your own selves shall men arise, speaking perverse things, to draw away disciples after them.

SIT.: This was Paul's farewell warning to the elders at Ephesus. CON.: Acts 20:17-38.

( ) **10. 1 Ne. 13:5**

Behold the foundation of a church which is most abominable above all other churches, which slayeth the saints of God, yea, and tortureth them and bindeth them down, and yoketh them with a yoke of iron, and bringeth them down into captivity.

SIT.: These words were spoken by an angel to Nephi as he was shown in vision the nations and kingdoms of the Gentiles. CON.: 1 Ne. 13:1-9. C.R.: 1 Ne. 13:26-29; 14:9-17; 22:13-23; 2 Ne. 6:12; 28:18-20; 2 Thess. 2:3-4; 1 Tim. 4:1-3; Rev. 13; 17; 18; D & C 18:20.

See "The Need for a Restoration—Bible Prophecies of the Apostasy," *The Prophecies of Joseph Smith,* pp. 191-196.

19. APOSTASY TAKING PLACE

( ) 1. 2 Pet. 2:1-2

There were false prophets also among the people,
even as there shall be false teachers among you,
who privily shall bring in damnable heresies, even
denying the Lord that brought them, and bring upon
themselves swift destruction. And many shall follow
their pernicious ways; by reason of whom the way
of truth shall be evil spoken of.

*SIT.: Peter has written that no prophecy of the
scripture is of any private interpretation because
they were spoken by the power of the Holy Ghost
by holy men of God. Then, as he acknowledges
that there were also false prophets in Old Testament times, he warns of evil teachers who would
also be found in the New Testament church. CON.:
2 Pet. 1:19-2:22.*

( ) 2. Gal. 1:6-7

I marvel that ye are so soon removed from him that
called you into the grace of Christ unto another gospel: Which is not another; but there be some that
trouble you, and would pervert the gospel of Christ.

( ) 3. Gal. 1:8-9

But though we, or an angel from heaven, preach any
other gospel unto you than that which we have
preached unto you, let him be accursed. As we said
before, so say I now again, If any man preach any
other gospel unto you than that ye have received,
let him be accursed.

*SIT.: Paul is warning the saints in Galatia that
there are those among them who are perverting
the gospel of Jesus Christ.*

( ) **4. Mt. 24:4-5**

Take heed that no man deceive you. For many shall
come in my name, saying, I am Christ; and shall deceive many.

*SIT.: Jesus gave this warning to his disciples
as he began his great sermon on the last days
which he gave on the Mt. of Olives. CON.: Mt.
24:1-12.*

( ) **5. Mt. 24:9-10**

Then shall they deliver you up to be afflicted, and
shall kill you; and ye shall be hated of all nations
for my name's sake. And then shall many be offended,
and shall betray one another, and shall hate one
another.

*SIT. Jesus gave this warning to his disciples as
he began his great sermon on the last days which
he gave on the Mt. of Olives. CON. Mt. 24:1-12.*

( ) **6. Mt. 7:15**

Beware of false prophets, which come to you in
sheep's clothing, but inwardly they are ravening
wolves.

*SIT.: Jesus gave this warning in his Sermon on
the Mount. CON Mt. 7:15-32.*

( ) **7. Jude 4**

There are certain men crept in unawares, who were

before of old ordained to this condemnation, ungodly men, turning the grace of our God into lasciviousness, and denying the only Lord God, and our Lord Jesus Christ.

SIT.: Jude's epistle is an admonition that the saints contend earnestly for the faith and not allow it to be altered by false teachers. CON.: Jude 3-8.

( ) **8. Rev. 2:4-5**

I have somewhat against thee, because thou hast left thy first love. Remember therefore from whence thou art fallen, and repent, and do the first works; or else I will come unto thee quickly, and will remove thy candlestick out of his place, except thou repent.

SIT.: This is the Lord's warning to the church at Ephesus. CON.: Rev. 2 1-7. NOTE: The branches of the church are represented as being candlesticks, the figure being that they are parts of the light of the world.

( ) **9. Jn. 16:2-3**

They shall put you out of the synagogues: yea, the time cometh, that whosoever killeth you will think that he doeth God service. And these things will they do unto you, because they have not known the Father, nor me.

SIT.: Jesus expressed this warning to his disciples while on the Mt. of Olives, shortly before his betrayal and arrest. CON.: Jn. 16:1-4.

( ) 10. Rev. 3:15-16

I know thy works, that thou art neither cold nor hot:
I would thou wert cold or hot. So then because thou
art lukewarm, and neither cold nor hot, I will spue
thee out of my mouth.

*SIT.: This is the Lord's warning to the church at
Laodicea. CON.: Rev. 3:14-21.*

20. EVENTS IN THE RESTORATION

Joseph Smith's First Vision

( ) **1. JS 2:17**

I saw two Personages, whose brightness and glory defy all description, standing above me in the air. One of them spake unto me, calling me by name and said, pointing to the other—*This is My Beloved Son. Hear Him!*

( ) **2. JS 2:18-19a**

I asked the Personages who stood above me in the light, which of all the sects was right—and which I should join. I was answered that I must join none of them, for they were all wrong; and the Personage who addressed me said that all their creeds were an abomination in his sight; that those professors were all corrupt; that:

( ) **3. JS 2:19b**

"They draw near to me with their lips, but their hearts are far from me, they teach for doctrines the commandments of men, having a form of godliness, but they deny the power thereof."

SIT.: This was Joseph Smith's description of his first vision which he received in the early spring of 1820. CON.: JS 2:10-20. C.R.: Is. 29:13; but Mt. 15:7-9.

The Coming of Moroni

( ) **4. JS 2:33**

He called me by name, and said unto me that he was

a messenger sent from the presence of God to me,
and that his name was Moroni; that God had a work
for me to do; and that my name should be had for
good and evil among all nations, kindreds, and
tongues, or that it should be both good and evil
spoken of among all people.

( ) **5. JS 2:34**

He said there was a book deposited, written upon
gold plates, giving an account of the former inhabitants of this continent, and the source from whence
they sprang. He also said that the fulness of the
everlasting Gospel was contained in it, as delivered
by the Savior to the ancient inhabitants.

*SIT.: The angel Moroni first came to Joseph Smith
on Sept. 21, 1823, to make known the location of
the Book of Mormon plates. CON.: JS 2:29-59.*

Receives Priesthood Authority
( ) **6. JS 2:72**

The messenger who visited us on this occasion and
conferred this Priesthood upon us, said that his name
was John, the same that is called John the Baptist
in the New Testament, and that he acted under the
direction of Peter, James and John, who held the
keys of the Priesthood of Melchizedek, which Priesthood, he said, would in due time be conferred on us.

*SIT.: John the Baptist appeared to Joseph Smith
and Oliver Cowdery on May 15, 1829. CON. JS
2 68 73. C R D & C 13.*

( ) 7. D & C 13

Upon you my fellow servants, in the name of Messiah I confer the Priesthood of Aaron, which holds the keys of the ministering of angels, and of the gospel of repentance, and of baptism by immersion for the remission of sins; and this shall never be taken again from the earth, until the sons of Levi do offer again an offering unto the Lord in righteousness.

SIT.: These words were spoken by John the Baptist as he conferred the priesthood upon Joseph Smith and Oliver Cowdery. C.R.: JS 2:68-73; D & C 84:18.

( ) 8. D & C 27:12

...Peter, and James, and John, whom I have sent unto you, by whom I have ordained you and confirmed you to be apostles, and especial witnesses of my name, and bear the keys of your ministry and of the same things which I revealed unto them.

SIT.: This reference to the ordaining of Joseph Smith (and Oliver Cowdery) to be apostles (and hence to the Melchizedek Priesthood) was made by the Lord in a revelation given to Joseph Smith in 1830. The Lord is promising Joseph that he will someday join with many great prophets on the earth in the last days. CON.: D & C 27:5-13.

( ) 9. D & C 20:1

The rise of the Church of Christ in these last days, being one thousand eight hundred and thirty years since the coming of our Lord and Savior Jesus Christ in the flesh, it being regularly organized and established agreeable to the laws of our country, by the will and commandments of God, in the fourth month, and on the sixth day of the month which is called April.

SIT.: This revelation was received through Joseph Smith shortly before the church was organized in April, 1830.

Appearances in the Kirtland Temple

( ) **10. D & C 110:1-16**

1. Christa - forgave sins, accepted the temple.
2. Moses - committed keys of the gathering of Israel and the leading of the ten tribes from the north.
3. Elias - committed the dispensation of the gospel of Abraham,
4. Elijah - committed the keys of this dispensation.

See ""The Church is Organized,"" *The Prophecies of Joseph Smith,* pp. 190-191.

21. BIBLE PROPHECIES OF
THE RESTORATION

( ) **1. Acts 3:19-21**

Your sins may be blotted out, when the times of re-
freshing shall come from the presence of the Lord;
And he shall send Jesus Christ, which before was
preached unto you: Whom the heaven must receive
until the times of restitution of all things.

> SIT.: *These references to the "times of refresh-
> ing" and "times of restitution of all things"
> were made by Peter as he addressed a group of
> people on Solomon's porch. CON.: Acts 3:11-23.
> C.R.: Eph. 1:10.*

( ) **2. Eph. 1:9-10**

[God has made] known unto us the mystery of his
will...That in the dispensation of the fulness of
times he might gather together in one all things in
Christ, both which are in heaven, and which are on
earth.

> SIT.: *Paul is discussing the nature of salvation
> which has been made available to man by God
> the Father and his son, Jesus Christ. CON.:
> Eph. 1:3-12.*

( ) **3. Dan. 2:44**

In the days of these kings shall the God of heaven
set up a kingdom, which shall never be destroyed:
and the kingdom shall not be left to other people,
but it shall break in pieces and consume all these
kingdoms, and it shall stand forever.

SIT.: This was Daniel's explanation of the stone which king Nebuchadnezzar saw break the image in his dream. CON.: the dream--Dan 2:31-35; the interpretation--Dan. 2:36-45. C.R.: D & C 65:2.

( ) **4. Tit. 2:13**

[We should be] Looking for that blessed hope, and the glorious appearing of the great God and our Saviour Jesus Christ.

USE: This scripture, which may be a reference to the coming of the Father and the Son to Joseph Smith in his first vision, is weakened by its ambiguity. Who is the great God? When else has he appeared with his son besides at the first vision given to Joseph Smith? FULFILLMENT JS 2:15-20.

( ) **5. Rev. 14:6-7**

I saw another angel fly in the midst of heaven, having the everlasting gospel to preach unto them that dwell on the earth, and to every nation, and kindred, and tongue, and people, Saying with a loud voice, Fear God, and give glory to him; for the hour of his judgment is come and worship him that made heaven, and earth, and the sea, and the fountains of waters.

USE This is understood to be a prophecy concerning the coming of Moroni to Joseph Smith. The Book of Mormon contains the fulness of the everlasting gospel (see JS 2:34. D & C 20:6:9, 27:5 42:12). C R D & C 133:36-39.

( ) **6. Mal. 3:1**

I will send my messenger, and he shall prepare the

way before me: and the Lord, whom ye seek, shall suddenly come to his temple, even the messenger of the covenant, whom ye delight in: behold, he shall come, saith the LORD of hosts.

> *CON.: Mal. 3:1-3. USE: This passage is a prophecy of the coming of John the Baptist, who was to prepare the way for the coming of the Lord. Note that the context shows that it will be Christ's coming in glory, when he will cleanse the earth, which the messenger is to precede. Use with Lk. 7:27-28. JS 2:68-73 gives the fulfillment. C.R.: Mt. 17:10-13; 11:10-14.*

( ) **7. Mal. 4:5-6**

I will send you Elijah the prophet before the coming of the great and dreadful day of the LORD: And he shall turn the heart of the fathers to the children, and the heart of the children to their fathers, lest I come and smite the earth with a curse.

> *FULFILLMENT: D & C 110:13-16. Elijah appeared to Joseph Smith and Oliver Cowdery in the Kirtland Temple and restored the keys of this dispensation. C.R.: JS 2:38-39.*

( ) **8. Mt. 24:14**

This gospel of the kingdom shall be preached in all the world for a witness unto all nations; and then shall the end come.

> *SIT.: Jesus made this prophecy to his disciples as he preached his great sermon on the last days. CON.: Mt. 24, 25.*

( ) **9. Is. 29:14**

I will proceed to do a marvellous work among this people, even a marvellous work and a wonder: for the wisdom of their wise men shall perish, and the understanding of their prudent men shall be hid.
>   CON.: Is. 29:9-14. USE: The marvellous work and a wonder is understood to be the restoration of the gospel. C.R.: =2 Ne. 27:26; 25:16-18; 1 Ne. 14:7; 22:8-11; 2 Ne. 29:1; 3 Ne. 21:9; 28:29-33; Morm. 8:34.

( ) **10. Mt. 16:19**

I will give unto thee the keys of the kingdom of heaven: and whatsoever thou shalt bind on earth shall be bound in heaven: and whatsoever thou shalt loose on earth shall be loosed in heaven.
>   SIT.: This promise was made to Peter by Jesus. CON.: Mt. 16:13-19. USE: What other church even claims to have the sealing powers (such as eternal marriage) here upon the earth? Yet we have them; see D & C 128:9-11.

See "The Restoration of Christ's Church Fulfills Prophecy," *The Prophecies of Joseph Smith,* pp. 190-202, where these and other prophecies of the restoration are explained and illustrated in charts.

22. BIBLE PROPHECIES OF THE BOOK OF MORMON

(   ) 1. **Ezek. 37:16-17**

Take thee one stick, and write upon it, For Judah, and for the children of Israel his companions: then take another stick, and write upon it, For Joseph, the stick of Ephraim, and for all the house of Israel his companions: And join them one to another into one stick; and they shall become one in thine hand.

SIT.: This revelation was given to Ezekiel by the Lord in connection with a prophecy concerning the gathering of Israel. It has often been abused by being taken out of context, for the context indicates that its ultimate fulfillment is yet future. CON.: Ezek. 37:15-28. C.R.: 2 Ne. 29: 13-14. See also 1 Ne. 5:14; Al. 10:3; D & C 19: 27, 27:5; and Journal of Discourses 23:184.

(   ) 2. **Gen. 49:22, 26**

Joseph is a fruitful bough, even a fruitful bough by a well; whose branches run over the wall:...The blessings of thy father have prevailed above the blessings of my progenitors unto the utmost bound of the everlasting hills: they shall be on the head of Joseph, and on the crown of the head of him that was separate from his brethren.

SIT.: This is a prophecy made by Jacob concerning the descendants of his son Joseph. CON.: Gen. 49:1, 22-26. NOTE: Branches = descendants; over the wall = cross the ocean; everlasting hills = the mountain chains which make up the continental divide in North, Central, and South America. C.R.: =Deut. 33:13-17.

( ) **3. Is. 29:1-6**

A prophecy of the fall of the Nephites:

Transition phrase: It shall be unto me as Ariel.
(Ariel is Jerusalem.)

1. The Lord shall camp against them round about.
2. They shall be brought down.
3. They shall speak out of the ground.
4. Their speech shall be as a familiar spirit.
5. Their destruction shall be at an instant, suddenly.

   SIT.: 2 Ne. 26:14-18 provides the interpretation that Isaiah is foretelling the fall of the Nephites by comparing their fall to the fall of Jerusalem. Mormon 6 shows the fulfillment.

( ) **4. Is. 29:11-12**

The vision of all is become unto you as the words of a book that is sealed, which men deliver to one that is learned, saying, Read this, I pray thee: and he saith, I cannot; for it is sealed: And the book is delivered to him that is not learned, saying, Read this, I pray thee: and he saith, I am not learned.

SIT.: Isaiah makes this prophecy to show that which will bring an end to the apostasy. CON.: Is. 29:9-14. FULFILLMENT: JS 2:63-65. Charles Anthon is understood to be the man that is learned; Joseph Smith is regarded as the man who is unlearned, although this is less certain. C.R.: 2 Ne. 27:15-22.

( ) **5. Ps. 85:11**

Truth shall spring out of the earth; and righteousness shall look down from heaven.

> NOTE: This is commonly interpreted as the Book
> of Mormon being taken from the earth while Mo-
> roni observed. See JS 2:59. C.R.: Is. 45:8.

( ) **6. Jn. 10:16**

Other sheep I have, which are not of this fold: them
also I must bring, and they shall hear my voice; and
there shall be one fold, and one shepherd.

> SIT.: Jesus said these words to a group of Phar-
> isees who were criticizing him. CON.: Jn. 9:40-
> 10:16. NOTE: When Jesus appeared in the Amer-
> icas he told the people that they were the other
> sheep; see 3 Ne. 15:11-24. The other sheep are
> not the gentiles--see Mt. 15:24. C.R.: D & C 10:
> 59-60.

( ) **7. 2 Cor. 13:1**

In the mouth of two or three witnesses shall every
word be established.

> USE: Another witness besides the Bible is there-
> fore needed. C.R.: 2 Ne. 29:6-10; Deut. 19:15.

( ) **8. Deut. 33:15-16**

[Joseph will be blessed] for the chief things of the
ancient mountains, and for the precious things of the
lasting hills. And for the precious things of the
earth and fulness thereof. and for the good will of
him that dwelt in the bush let the blessing come up
on the head of Joseph, and upon the top of the head
of him that was separated from his brethren.

> SIT.: Moses repeated the blessings of Jacob up

on the tribes of Israel. *CON.: Deut. 33:1, 13-17.*
C.R.: Gen. 49:22-26.

( ) 9. Rev. 22:18-19

I testify unto every man that heareth the words of
the prophecy of this book, If any man shall add unto
these things, God shall add unto him the plagues
that are written in this book: And if any man shall
take away from the words of the book of this prophecy, God shall take away his part out of the book
of life, and out of the holy city, and from the things
which are written in this book.

SIT.: This was John's final admonition as he
closed the book of Revelation. Some people use
this to mean that there can be no more scripture
besides the Bible. John could only have meant
Revelation and not the Bible, for the Bible was
not yet compiled at that time. His other Bible
books (the Gospel of John, I John, II John, III
John) were probably written after Revelation was
written, also. See also Deut. 4:2.

( ) 10. Gen. 11:8

So the LORD scattered them abroad from thence upon the face of all the earth: and they left off to build
the city.

SIT.: The Lord scattered the people who were
building the tower of Babel. It was at this time
the Jaredites came to the Americas. CON.: Gen.
11:1-9. C.R.: Eth. 1:33-43.

See "Prophecies Concerning the Book of Mormon,"
The Prophecies of Joseph Smith, pp. 155-189, for a
detailed explanation of these and other related prophecies.

23. BOOK OF MORMON PROPHECIES OF ITS RESTORATION

( ) **1. 2 Ne. 3:7, 15**

A choice seer will I raise up out of the fruit of thy loins; and he shall be esteemed highly among the fruit of thy loins...And his name shall be called after me; and it shall be after the name of his father. And he shall be like unto me; for the thing, which the Lord shall bring forth by his hand, by the power of the Lord shall bring my people unto salvation.

SIT.: Lehi was quoting prophecies made by Joseph who was sold into Egypt to his son, Joseph. The Joseph who was sold into Egypt prophesied of a man who would have his name and whose father would also have his name: Joseph Smith. CON.: 2 Ne. 3:4-21.

( ) **2. 2 Ne. 27:9-10**

The book shall be delivered unto a man, and he shall deliver the words of the book, which are the words of those who have slumbered in the dust, and he shall deliver these words unto another: But the words which are sealed he shall not deliver, neither shall he deliver the book.

( ) **3. 2 Ne. 27:15, 17-18**

The Lord God shall say unto him to whom he shall deliver the book: Take these words which are not sealed and deliver them to another, that he may show them unto the learned, saying: Read this, I pray thee. And the learned shall say: Bring hither the book, and I will read them...And the man shall say: I cannot bring the book, for it is sealed. Then shall the learned say: I cannot read it.

SIT.: This is Nephi's prophecy of the Martin Harris—Charles Anthon incident; see JS 2:63-65. CON.: 2 Ne. 27:6-20. C.R.: Is. 29:11-12.

( ) 4. 2 Ne. 27:12-13

The book shall be hid from the eyes of the world, that the eyes of none shall behold it save it be that three witnesses shall behold it, by the power of God, besides him to whom the book shall be delivered; and they shall testify to the truth of the book and the things therein. And there is none other which shall view it, save it be a few according to the will of God.

SIT.: This is Nephi's prophecy of the three and the eight witnesses. See their testimonies in the front of the Book of Mormon. CON.: 2 Ne. 27: 11-14.

( ) 5. 2 Ne. 26:15-18

A prophecy of the fall of the Nephites:

1. The Lord shall camp against them round about.
2. They shall be brought low in the dust, until they are not.
3. Those who are destroyed shall speak out of the ground.
4. Their speech shall be as a familiar spirit.
5. Their destruction shall be at an instant, suddenly.

SIT.: Nephi is expounding on the prophecy of

Is. 29:1-6. He shows that Isaiah's prophecy is comparing the fall of Jerusalem (Ariel) with the fall of the Nephites. CON.: 2 Ne. 26:14-21. C.R.: Morm. 6; Is. 29:1-6.

( ) **6. 3 Ne. 15:21-22**

Ye are they of whom I said: Other sheep I have which are not of this fold; them also I must bring, and they shall hear my voice; and there shall be one fold, and one shepherd. And they understood me not, for they supposed it had been the Gentiles; for they understood not that the Gentiles should be converted through their preaching.

SIT.: The resurrected Christ is teaching the Nephites in the Americas. CON.: 3 Ne. 15:11-16:5. C.R.: Jn. 10:14-16; Mt. 15:24; D & C 10:59-60.

( ) **7. Moro. 10:27-28**

The time speedily cometh that ye shall know that I lie not, for ye shall see me at the bar of God; and the Lord God will say unto you: Did I not declare my words unto you, which were written by this man, like as one crying from the dead, yea, even as one speaking out of the dust? I declare these things unto the fulfilling of the prophecies.

SIT.: This was the warning given by Moroni to those who will read the Book of Mormon in the last days. CON.: Moro. 10:1-30.

( ) **8. 2 Ne. 27:22**

When thou hast read the words which I have commanded thee, and obtained the witnesses which I have promised unto thee, then shalt thou seal up the book again, and hide it up unto me, that I may preserve the words which thou hast not read, until I shall see fit in mine own wisdom to reveal all things unto the children of men.

SIT.: This is Nephi's prophecy of the words of the Lord to Joseph Smith in the period he was to be translating the Book of Mormon. CON.: 2 Ne. 27:20-23. FULFILLMENT: JS 2:60.

( ) **9. Morm. 8:28**

[The Book of Mormon] shall come in a day when the power of God shall be denied, and churches become defiled and be lifted up in the pride of their hearts; yea, even in a day when leaders of churches and teachers shall rise in the pride of their hearts, even to the envying of them who belong to their churches.

SIT.: Moroni is prophesying concerning the world conditions when the Book of Mormon is to be re- stored. CON.: Morm. 8:26-41.

( ) **10. 2 Ne. 28:3-4**

It shall come to pass in that day that the churches which are built up, and not unto the Lord, when the one shall say unto the other: Behold, I, I am the Lord's; and the others shall say: I, I am the Lord's; and thus shall every one say that hath built up chur- ches, and not unto the Lord—And they shall contend one with another; and their priests shall contend one with another, and they shall teach with their learn- ing, and deny the Holy Ghost, which giveth utter- ance.

SIT.: Nephi is prophesying concerning the condition of the churches when the Book of Mormon is to be restored. CON.: 2 Ne. 28:3-14.

See "The Witnesses to The Book of Mormon Fulfill Ancient and Modern Prophecy," *The Prophecies of Joseph Smith,* pp. 128-154, for a detailed explanation of these and other related prophecies.

24. MISSION OF THE BOOK OF MORMON

( ) **1. Acts 10:34-35**

God is no respecter of persons: But in every nation he that feareth him, and worketh righteousness, is accepted with him.

SIT.: Peter is speaking to Cornelius, a Roman centurion. He has seen that the Holy Ghost has been poured out upon the man's household. CON.: Acts 10:1-48. C.R.: 2 Chron. 19:7; Deut. 10:17; Ro. 2:11; Gal. 2:6; Eph. 6:9; Col. 3:25. USE: This passage shows that if God will bless one group with his scriptures, he will bless other groups in a similar manner.

( ) **2. 1 Ne. 13:40**

These last records...shall establish the truth of the first, which are of the twelve apostles of the Lamb, and shall make known the plain and precious things which have been taken away from them; and shall make known to all kindreds, tongues, and people, that the Lamb of God is the Son of the Eternal Father, and the Savior of the world; and that all men must come unto him, or they cannot be saved.

SIT.: These words were spoken to Nephi by an angel, who had revealed to him the coming forth of the Book of Mormon. CON.: 1 Ne. 13:38-42.

( ) **3. Morm. 5:14**

[The Book of Mormon] shall go unto the unbelieving of the Jews; and for this intent shall they go—that

they may be persuaded that Jesus is the Christ, the
Son of the living God; that the Father may bring a-
bout, through his most Beloved, his great and eternal purpose, in restoring the Jews, or all the house
of Israel, to the land of their inheritance.

*SIT.: Mormon is explaining the purpose for the
abridgment he is making of the Book of Mormon
plates. CON.: Morm. 5:8-15.*

( ) **4. 2 Ne. 33:10**

Hearken unto these words and believe in Christ; and
if ye believe not in these words believe in Christ.
And if ye shall believe in Christ ye will believe in
these words, for they are the words of Christ, and
he hath given them unto me; and they teach all men
that they should do good.

*SIT.: Nephi bears this witness in his parting tes-
timony.*

( ) **5. Morm. 7:8-9**

Lay hold upon the gospel of Christ, which shall be
set before you, not only in this record but also in
the record which shall come unto the Gentiles from
the Jews, which record shall come from the Gentiles
unto you. For behold, this is written for the intent
that ye may believe that; and if ye believe that ye
will believe this also.

*SIT.: Mormon is writing to the remnant of the peo-
ple who survived the final war between the Nephites and the Lamanites.*

( ) **6. 2 Ne. 29:8**

Know ye not that the testimony of two nations is a

witness unto you that I am God, that I remember one nation like unto another? Wherefore, I speak the same words unto one nation like unto another. And when the two nations shall run together the testimony of the two nations shall run together also.

SIT.: Nephi is prophesying the reaction of many of the Gentiles to the Book of Mormon when it comes forth. CON.: 2 Ne. 29:3-14.

( ) **7. 2 Ne. 27:6-7**

It shall come to pass that the Lord God shall bring forth unto you the words of a book, and they shall be the words of them which have slumbered. And behold the book shall be sealed; and in the book shall be a revelation from God, from the beginning of the world to the ending thereof.

SIT.: Nephi is prophesying concerning the coming forth of the Book of Mormon. CON.: 2 Ne. 27:6-22. C.R.: Eth. 3:25-27; 4:1-7.

( ) **8. 2 Ne. 3:12**

That which shall be written by the fruit of thy loins, and also that which shall be written by the fruit of the loins of Judah, shall grow together, unto the confounding of false doctrines and laying down of contentions, and establishing peace among the fruit of thy loins, and bringing them to the knowledge of their fathers in the latter days, and also to the knowledge of my covenants, saith the Lord.

SIT.: Lehi is quoting a revelation given by the Lord to Joseph who was sold into Egypt. CON.: 2 Ne. 3:5-16.

( ) 9. D & C 3:18

This testimony shall come to the knowledge of the Lamanites, and the Lemuelites, and the Ishmaelites, who dwindled in unbelief because of the iniquity of their fathers, whom the Lord has suffered to destroy their brethren the Nephites, because of their iniquities and their abominations.

> *SIT.: This revelation was given to Joseph Smith in 1828 and pertained to the 116 pages of the Book of Mormon manuscript which were lost. CON.: D & C 3:16-20.*

( ) 10. Eth. 5:4

In the mouth of three witnesses shall these things be established; and the testimony of three, and this work, in the which shall be shown forth the power of God and also his word, of which the Father, and the Son, and the Holy Ghost bear record—and all this shall stand as a testimony against the world at the last day.

> *SIT.: Moroni is writing to the future translator of his writings.*

25. THE ARTICLES OF FAITH

Several slightly varying lists of the principles of the church, or articles of faith, are found in the early publications of the church. The list which is now a portion of the Pearl of Great Price was written by Joseph Smith for a newspaper editor, Mr. John Wentworth, on March 1, 1842. See *History of the Church* 4:535-541.

1. Article of Faith 1

We believe in God, the Eternal Father, and in His son, Jesus Christ, and in the Holy Ghost.

2. Article of Faith 2

We believe that men will be punished for their own sins, and not for Adam's transgression.

3. Article of Faith 3

We believe that through the Atonement of Christ, all mankind may be saved, by obedience to the laws and ordinances of the Gospel.

4. Article of Faith 4

We believe that the first principles and ordinances of the Gospel are: first, Faith in the Lord Jesus Christ; second, Repentance; third, Baptism by immersion for the remission of sins; fourth, Laying on of hands for the gift of the Holy Ghost.

5. Article of Faith 5

We believe that a man must be called of God, by pro-

THE ARTICLES OF FAITH

phecy, and by the laying on of hands, by those who are in authority to preach the Gospel and administer in the ordinances thereof.

6. Article of Faith 6

We believe in the same organization that existed in the Primitive Church, viz.,[1] apostles, prophets, pastors, teachers, evangelists, etc.

7. Article of Faith 7

We believe in the gift of tongues, prophecy, revelation, visions, healing, interpretation of tongues, etc.

8. Article of Faith 8

We believe the Bible to be the word of God as far as it is translated correctly; we also believe the Book of Mormon to be the word of God.

9. Article of Faith 9

We believe all that God has revealed, all that He does now reveal, and we believe that He will yet reveal many great and important things pertaining to the Kingdom of God.

10. Article of Faith 10

We believe in the literal gathering of Israel and in the restoration of the Ten Tribes; that Zion will be built upon this [the American] continent; that Christ will reign personally upon the earth; and, that the earth will be renewed and receive its paradisiacal glory.

---

[1]Say "namely."

11. Article of Faith 11

We claim the privilege of worshiping Almighty God according to the dictates of our own conscience, and allow all men the same privilege, let them worship how, where, or what they may.

12. Article of Faith 12

We believe in being subject to kings, presidents, rulers, and magistrates, in obeying, honoring, and sustaining the law.

13. Article of Faith 13

We believe in being honest, true, chaste, benevolent, virtuous, and in doing good to all men; indeed, we may say that we follow the admonition of Paul—We believe all things, we hope all things, we have endured many things, and hope to be able to endure all things. If there is anything virtuous, lovely, or of good report or praiseworthy, we seek after these things.

26. ONLY ONE AUTHORIZED CHURCH

( ) 1. **Mt. 7:21**

Not every one that saith unto me, Lord, Lord, shall enter into the kingdom of heaven; but he that doeth the will of my Father which is in heaven.

( ) 2. **Mt. 7:22-23**

Many will say to me in that day, Lord, Lord, have we not prophesied in thy name? and in thy name have cast out devils? and in thy name done many wonderful works? And then will I profess unto them, I never knew you: depart from me, ye that work iniquity.

SIT.: Jesus said these words in his Sermon on the Mount as he warned his disciples against false prophets. CON.: Mt. 7:13-23.

( ) 3. **Eph. 4:5**

One Lord, one faith, one baptism.

SIT.: Paul is striving for unity within the church. CON.: Eph. 4:4-6, 11-14.

( ) 4. **1 Cor. 1:13**

Is Christ divided? was Paul crucified for you? or were ye baptized in the name of Paul?

SIT.: Paul is admonishing the saints to put away divisions and all speak the same thing. CON.: 1 Cor. 1:10-13.

( ) **5. Mt. 18:17**

If he shall neglect to hear them, tell it unto the church: but if he neglect to hear the church, let him be unto thee as an heathen man and a publican.

SIT.: Jesus is instructing his disciples how to handle disputes in the church, saying that one's brother should hear witnesses privately first, and then, if necessary, the matter should be taken to the church. CON.: Mt. 18:15-22. USE: This passage is evidence that Christ's church was organized and functioning while the Savior was still upon the earth.

( ) **6. D & C 38:27**

I say unto you, be one; and if ye are not one ye are not mine.

SIT.: This revelation was given through Joseph Smith to the church in 1831. CON.: D & C 38:24-27.

( ) **7. D & C 1:30**

Those to whom these commandments were given, might have power to lay the foundation of this church, and to bring it forth out of obscurity and out of darkness, the only true and living church upon the face of the whole earth, with which I, the Lord, am well pleased, speaking unto the church collectively and not individually.

SIT.: In this revelation, which was given through Joseph Smith to elders of the church in 1831, the Lord is listing the purposes for the command-

ments which he has revealed.   CON.: D & C
1:24-30.

( ) **8. 3 Ne. 27:8**

How be it my church save it be called in my name?
For if a church be called in Moses' name then it be
Moses' church; or if it be called in the name of a
man then it be the church of a man; but if it be
called in my name then it is my church, if it so be
that they are built upon my gospel.

*SIT.: The resurrected Christ appeared to his
disciples in the Americas in response to their
prayer. They asked him what his church was to
be called. CON.: 3 Ne. 27:1-10.*

( ) **9. D & C 71:9-10**

There is no weapon that is formed against you shall
prosper; And if any man lift his voice against you
he shall be confounded in mine own due time.

*SIT.: This revelation was given to Joseph Smith
and Sidney Rigdon in 1831. CON.: D & C 71:7-10.*

( ) **10. D & C 84:65-73**

These signs shall follow them that believe—In my
name they shall do many wonderful works.

    1. cast out devils
    2. heal the sick
    3. open the eyes of the blind
    4. unstop the ears of the deaf
    5. make the dumb speak
    6. poison shall not hurt them
    7. they shall not boast of these things.

SIT.: This revelation was given through Joseph Smith to elders of the church in 1832. C.R.: Mk. 16:17-18.

See "The Savior's Prophetic Promises Fulfilled— Miracles and Persecution," *The Prophecies of Joseph Smith,* pp. 289-307.

27. AUTHORITY IN THE MINISTRY

( ) **1. Jn. 15:16**

Ye have not chosen me, but I have chosen you, and ordained you, that ye should go and bring forth fruit.

SIT.: Jesus said these words to his apostles as he explained their relationship on the Mt. of Olives, just before his betrayal and arrest. CON.: Jn. 15:1-16. C.R.: Mk. 3:14-21; Mt. 10:1-4; Lk. 6:13-16.

( ) **2. Mt. 10:1**

When he had called unto him his twelve disciples, he gave them power against unclean spirits, to cast them out, and to heal all manner of sickness and all manner of disease.

CON.: Mt. 10:1-42. C.R.: Jn. 15:16; Mk. 3:14-21; Lk. 6:13-16.

( ) **3. Ro. 10:15**

How shall they preach, except they be sent?

CON.: Ro. 10:14-16. C.R.: Jn. 15:16; Heb. 5:4.

( ) **4. Heb. 5:4**

No man taketh this honour unto himself, but he that is called of God, as was Aaron.

SIT.: Paul is discussing the nature of a priesthood calling. CON.: Heb. 5:1-10. C.R.: Ex. 28:1, 3, 41; 40:13-15.

( ) 5. **Ex. 28:1, 3, 41**

The calling of Aaron:

1. Take thou unto thee Aaron thy brother...(revelation to one in authority)
2. Thou shalt speak unto all that are wise hearted... (sustained by the congregation)
3. Thou shalt anoint them, and consecrate them, and sanctify them...(an O.T. form of ordination)

   SIT.: This is the calling of Aaron and his sons. CON.: Ex. 28:1-43. USE: the length of this passage makes its use difficult. It is often better to precede it with Num. 27:18-23, in which the form is more clearly shown.

( ) 6. **Num. 27:18-23**

The calling of Joshua:

1. The LORD said unto Moses, Take thee Joshua... (revelation to one in authority)
2. Moses set Joshua before Eleazar the priest, and before all the congregation...(sustained by the congregation)
3. Moses laid his hands upon him, and gave him a charge, as the LORD commanded by the hand of Moses...(ordination)

   SIT.: The Lord was ready to take Moses from the earth and preparations were being made for a new leader for the children of Israel. CON.: Num. 27:15-23.

( ) 7. **D & C 42:11**

It shall not be given to any one to go forth to preach

my gospel, or to build up my church, except he be ordained by some one who has authority, and it is known to the church that he has authority and has been regularly ordained by the heads of the church.

SIT.: This revelation was given through Joseph Smith to elders of the church in 1831. CON.: D & C 42:11-17. C.R.: D & C 11:15-17.

( ) 8. Acts 6:1-6
The calling of the seven deacons:

1. The twelve told the multitude to "look ye out among you seven men of honest report, full of the Holy Ghost and wisdom." (command by those in authority)
2. The saying pleased the whole multitude, and they chose seven. (sustained by the congregation)
3. The seven were set before the apostles, "and when they had prayed, they laid their hands on them." (ordination)

SIT.: This took place in Jerusalem.

( ) 9. Acts 13:1-3
The mission call of Barnabas and Paul:

1. There were prophets and teachers. As they ministered to the Lord "the Holy Ghost said, Separate me Barnabas and Saul for the work whereunto I have called them." (revelation to those in authority)
2. "When they had fasted and prayed, and laid their hands on them, they sent them away." (ordination or setting apart)

SIT.: This took place at Antioch.

( ) **10. Acts 19:1-6**

Rebaptism by one having authority:

1. Paul found disciples who hadn't even heard that the Holy Ghost existed.
2. They claimed that they were baptized with the baptism of John.
3. Paul knew that the baptism was performed by someone without authority, for John the Baptist taught that following his baptism Jesus would come to baptize them with the Holy Ghost.
4. "When they heard this, they were baptized in the name of the Lord Jesus. And when Paul had laid his hands upon them, the Holy Ghost came on them; and they spake with tongues, and prophesied."

SIT.: Paul encountered this situation at Ephesus.

28. CHURCH ORGANIZATION

( ) **1. Eph. 2:19-21**

Ye are...of the household of God; And are built upon
the foundation of the apostles and prophets, Jesus
Christ himself being the chief corner stone; In whom
all the building fitly framed together groweth unto
an holy temple in the Lord.

*SIT.: Paul was stressing the unity of the church
to the saints in Ephesus.*

( ) **2. Eph. 4:11**

He gave some, apostles; and some, prophets; and
some, evangelists; and some, pastors and teachers...

*SIT.: Paul was stressing the unity of the church
to the saints at Ephesus. CON.: Eph. 4:4-6,11-14.*

( ) **3. Heb. 5:1**

Every high priest taken from among men is ordained
for men in things pertaining to God, that he may offer both gifts and sacrifices for sins.

*SIT.: Paul made this reference to the office of
high priest as he said that this was the office
which Jesus held in the Melchizedek priesthood.
CON.: Heb. 5:1-10.*

( ) **4. Lk. 10:1, 17**

The Lord appointed other seventy also, and sent
them two and two before his face into every city and
place, whither he himself would come...And the
seventy returned again with joy, saying, Lord, even

the devils are subject unto us through thy name.
CON.: Lk. 10:1-24.

( ) **5. Acts 14:23**

When they had ordained them elders in every church,
and had prayed with fasting, they commended them
to the Lord, on whom they believed.

*SIT.: These ordinations were performed by Paul
and Barnabas in Lystra, Iconium, and Antioch.
CON.: Acts 14:21-23.*

( ) **6. 1 Tim. 3:2**

A bishop then must be blameless, the husband of
one wife, vigilant, sober, of good behaviour, given
to hospitality, apt to teach.

*SIT.: Paul is outlining the qualifications for the
office of bishop. CON.: 1 Tim. 3:1-7.*

( ) **7. 1 Tim. 3:8-9**

Likewise must the deacons be grave, not double-
tongued, not given to much wine, not greedy of filthy
lucre; Holding the mystery of the faith in a pure
conscience.

*SIT.: Paul is outlining the qualifications for the
office of deacon. CON.: 1 Tim. 3:8-13.*

( ) **8. Acts 1:23-26**

The choosing of Matthias for the apostleship:

1. The church met to choose another apostle to fill
   the vacancy left by Judas.
2. They appointed two candidates Joseph and

Matthias.

3. They prayed, saying, "Thou, Lord, which knowest the hearts of all men, shew whether of these two thou hast chosen..."

4. "They gave forth their lots; and the lot fell upon Matthias; and he was numbered with the eleven apostles."

CON.: Acts 1:15-26.

( ) **9. Acts 19:13-16**

The unauthorized ministrations of the sons of Sceva:

1. The seven sons of Sceva, who were vagabond Jews and exorcists, attempted to cast out evil spirits in the name of Jesus.

2. The evil spirit called out, "Jesus I know, and Paul I know; but who are ye?"

3. The man possessed of the evil spirit then attacked them and drove the seven sons from the house naked and wounded.

SIT.: This took place at Ephesus during Paul's third missionary journey.

( ) **10. Heb. 5:10**

⌈Christ is⌉ Called of God an high priest after the order of Melchisedec.

SIT.: Paul is explaining the nature of Jesus' authority.   CON.: Heb. 5:1-10.   C.R.: Gen. 14:18-20; Heb. 7:1-3; D & C 107:1-3; 84:14, 17; Al. 13:7-9.

29. DUTIES OF PRIESTHOOD OFFICIALS

( ) **1. D & C 107:3**

The Holy Priesthood, after the Order of the Son of God.

    SIT.: This revelation, given through Joseph Smith to the twelve apostles, gives the true name of the higher priesthood. CON.: D & C 107:1-4. C.R.: Al. 13:1-15; Moses 8:19; 6:7.

( ) **2. D & C 107:8**

The Melchizedek Priesthood holds the right of presidency, and has power and authority over all the offices in the church in all ages of the world, to administer in spiritual things.

    CON.: D & C 107:6-12,18-20.

( ) **3. D & C 107:20**

The power and authority of the lesser, or Aaronic Priesthood, is to hold the keys of the ministering of angels, and to administer in outward ordinances, the letter of the gospel, the baptism of repentance for the remission of sins, agreeable to the covenants and commandments.

    CON.: D & C 107:13-16.

( ) **4. D & C 20:60**

Every elder, priest, teacher, or deacon is to be ordained according to the gifts and callings of God unto him; and he is to be ordained by the power of the Holy Ghost, which is in the one who ordains him.

SIT.: This revelation was given through Joseph Smith just before the church was organized in April, 1830.

( ) **5. D & C 20:38-45**
Duties of the elders:

1. Baptize
2. Ordain other elders, priests, teachers, and deacons
3. Administer the sacrament
4. Confirm those who are baptized into the church
5. Teach, expound, and exhort
6. Watch over the church
7. Take the lead of meetings, as they are led by the Holy Ghost

( ) **6. D & C 20:46-52**
Duties of priests:

1. Preach, teach, expound, exhort
2. Baptize
3. Administer the sacrament
4. Visit the house of each member, and exhort them to pray and attend to family duties
5. Ordain priests, teachers, and deacons
6. Take the lead of meetings when no elder is present
7. Assist the elders if the occasion arises

( ) **7. D & C 20:53-59**

Duties of teachers and deacons:

1. Watch over the church always
2. Be with and strengthen the church
3. See that there is no iniquity, hardness, lying, backbiting, nor evil speaking in the church
4. See that the church meets together often
5. See that all the members do their duty
6. Take the lead in the absence of the elder or priest
7. Warn, expound, exhort and teach, and invite all to come to Christ
8. The teacher is to be assisted in all his duties in the church by the deacons, if the occasion requires

( ) **8. D & C 107:25**

The Seventy are also called to preach the gospel, and to be especial witnesses unto the Gentiles and in all the world—thus differing from other officers in the church in the duties of their calling.

CON.· D & C 107:25-32.

( ) **9. D & C 107:10**

High priests after the order of the Melchizedek Priesthood have a right to officiate in their own standing, under the direction of the presidency, in administering spiritual things, and also in the office of an elder, priest (of the Levitical order), teacher, deacon, and member.

( ) 10. D & C 107:23-24

The twelve traveling councilors are called to be the Twelve Apostles, or special witnesses of the name of Christ in all the world—thus differing from other officers in the church in the duties of their calling. And they form a quorum, equal in authority and power to the three presidents previously mentioned.

CON.: D & C 107:21-32.

ᵤee Part V, "Gifts of Church Administration," *Gifts of The Spirit*, pp. 275-301. These three chapters treat the gifts of administration, diversities of operations, and the discerning of spirits.

30. USE OF PRIESTHOOD AUTHORITY

( ) 1. D & C 121:34-35a

There are many called, but few are chosen. And why are they not chosen? Because their hearts are set so much upon the things of this world, and aspire to the honors of men,...

( ) 2. D & C 121:35b-36

(that) they do not learn this one lesson—That the rights of the priesthood are inseparably connected with the powers of heaven, and that the powers of heaven cannot be controlled nor handled only upon the principles of righteousness.

( ) 3. D & C 121:37

That they may be conferred upon us, it is true; but when we undertake to cover our sins, or to gratify our pride, our vain ambition, or to exercise control or dominion or compulsion upon the souls of the children of men, in any degree of unrighteousness, behold, the heavens withdraw themselves, the Spirit of the Lord is grieved; and when it is withdrawn, Amen to the priesthood or the authority of that man.

SIT.: This revelation was given in answer to the prayer of Joseph Smith while he and his companions were imprisoned in Liberty Jail in 1839. CON.: D & C 121:34-46. C.R.: Mt. 20:1-16; 22:1-14; D & C 95:5-6; 105:35-36.

( ) 4. **D & C 107:22**

Three Presiding High Priests, chosen by the body, appointed and ordained to that office, and upheld by the confidence, faith, and prayer of the church, form a quorum of the Presidency of the Church.

CON.: D & C 107:22-32.

( ) 5. **D & C 107:18-19**

The power and authority of the higher, or Melchizedek Priesthood, is to hold the keys of all the spiritual blessings of the church—To have the privilege of receiving the mysteries of the kingdom of heaven, to have the heavens opened unto them, to commune with the general assembly and church of the Firstborn, and to enjoy the communion and presence of God the Father, and Jesus the mediator of the new covenant.

C.R.: D & C 84:19-22.

( ) 6. **D & C 84:39-40**

This is according to the oath and covenant which belongeth to the priesthood. Therefore, all those who receive the priesthood, receive this oath and covenant of my Father, which he cannot break, neither can it be moved.

CON.: D & C 84:31-42.

( ) 7. **D & C 84:20-21**

In the ordinances thereof, the power of godliness is manifest. And without the ordinances thereof, and the authority of the priesthood, the power of godliness is not manifest unto men in the flesh.

SIT.: In this important revelation on priesthood the Lord revealed through Joseph Smith the lineage of the priesthood from Adam to Moses and then explained a portion of the priesthood calling. This passage has reference to the ordinances of the Melchizedek priesthood. CON.: D & C 84:19-25.

( ) **8. D & C 107:27-28**

Every decision made by either of these quorums must be by the unanimous voice of the same; that is. every member in each quorum must be agreed to its decisions, in order to make their decisions of the same power or validity one with the other—A majority may form a quorum when circumstances render it impossible to be otherwise.

SIT.: This passage has reference to decisions made by the First Presidency and the Quorum of the Twelve. CON.: D & C 107:21-32.

( ) **9. D & C 107:30**

The decisions of these quorums, or either of them, are to be made in all righteousness, in holiness, and lowliness of heart, meekness and long suffering, and in faith, and virtue, and knowledge, temperance, patience, godliness, brotherly kindness and charity.

SIT.: This passage has reference to decisions made by the First Presidency and the Quorum of the Twelve. CON.: D & C 107:21-32.

( ) **10. D & C 38:42**

Go ye out from among the wicked. Save yourselves. Be ye clean that bear the vessels of the Lord.

SIT.: This revelation was given through Joseph Smith to the church in 1831. CON.: D & C 38:40-42.

31. THE PRIESTHOOD ORDINANCES

( ) **1. D & C 20:73**

Having been commissioned of Jesus Christ, I baptize you in the name of the Father, and of the Son, and of the Holy Ghost. Amen.

SIT.: This is the baptismal prayer. It was revealed through Joseph Smith just prior to the organization of the church in April, 1830. CON.: D & C 20:37,68-74. C.R.: 3 Ne. 11:21-28; Mos. 18:8-15; Moro. 6:1-4.

( ) **2. D & C 39:23**

On as many as ye shall baptize with water, ye shall lay your hands, and they shall receive the gift of the Holy Ghost, and shall be looking forth for the signs of my coming, and shall know me.

SIT.: This revelation was given through Joseph Smith to James Covill in 1831. CON.: D & C 39:20-23. C.R.: D & C 33:15; 20:68.

( ) **3. D & C 20:77**

O God, the Eternal Father, we ask thee in the name of thy Son, Jesus Christ, to bless and sanctify this bread to the souls of all those who partake of it, that they may eat in remembrance of the body of thy Son, and witness unto thee, O God, the Eternal Father, that they are willing to take upon them the name of thy Son, and always remember him and keep his commandments which he has given them; that they may always have his Spirit to be with them. Amen.

SIT.: This is the sacramental prayer on the bread. It was revealed through Joseph Smith just prior to the organization of the church in April, 1830. CON.: D & C 20:75-79. C.R.: Moro. 4:1-3.

( ) 4. D & C 20:79

O God, the Eternal Father, we ask thee in the name of thy Son, Jesus Christ, to bless and sanctify this water to the souls of all those who drink of it, that they may do it in remembrance of the blood of thy Son, which was shed for them; that they may witness unto thee, O God, the Eternal Father, that they do always remember him, that they may have his Spirit to be with them. Amen.

SIT.: This is the sacramental prayer on the water. The revelation as it is given reads wine, but it is given above as water in accordance with the current practice of the church. See D & C 27:1-4. CON.: D & C 20:75-79. C.R.: Moro. 5:1-2.

( ) 5. D & C 20:70

Every member of the church of Christ having children is to bring them unto the elders before the church, who are to lay their hands upon them in the name of Jesus Christ, and bless them in his name.

C.R.: 3 Ne. 17:21-25; 26:14-16; Mk. 10:13-16; Mt. 18:1-6.

( ) **6. D & C 42:44**

The elders of the church, two or more, shall be
called, and shall pray for and lay their hands upon
them in my name; and if they die they shall die unto
me, and if they live they shall live unto me.

*SIT.: In this revelation, given through Joseph
Smith in 1831 to elders of the church, the Lord
revealed the law of his church. CON.: D & C
42:43-52. C.R.: Jas. 5:14-15.*

( ) **7. Jas. 5:14-15**

Is any sick among you? let him call for the elders
of the church; and let them pray over him, anointing
him with oil in the name of the Lord: And the prayer
of faith shall save the sick, and the Lord shall
raise him up; and if he have committed sins, they
shall be forgiven him.

*SIT.: James is instructing the church on the
value of prayer. CON.: Jas. 5:13-18.*

( ) **8. D & C 28:13**

All things must be done in order, and by common
consent in the church, by the prayer of faith.

*SIT.: This revelation was given through Joseph
Smith to Oliver Cowdery in 1830. Oliver was to
speak to Hiram Page, who had been receiving
spurious commandments through a peep stone,
and tell him that he had been deceived. CON.:
D & C 28:12-14. C.R.: D & C 20:63, 65-66;
26:2; 28:13.*

( ) **9. D & C 132:45**

I have conferred upon you the keys and power of the priesthood, wherein I restore all things, and make known unto you all things in due time.

( ) **10. D & C 132:46**

And verily, verily, I say unto you, that whatsoever you seal on earth shall be sealed in heaven; and whatsoever you bind on earth, in my name and by my word, saith the Lord, it shall be eternally bound in the heavens; and whosesoever sins you remit on earth shall be remitted eternally in the heavens; and whosesoever sins you retain on earth shall be retained in heaven.

SIT.: This revelation and promise was given to Joseph Smith by revelation in connection with the eternal marriage principle. CON.: D & C 132:45-48. C.R.: D & C 128:7-11; Mt. 16:18-19.

32. PREPARATORY GOSPEL DEFINED

( ) **1. D & C 39:6**

This is my gospel—repentance and baptism by water, and then cometh the baptism of fire and the Holy Ghost, even the Comforter, which showeth all things, and teacheth the peaceable things of the kingdom.

SIT.: This revelation was given through Joseph Smith to James Covill in 1831. CON.: D & C 33: 8-12.

( ) **2. D & C 33:11-12**

Repent and be baptized, every one of you, for a remission of your sins; yea, be baptized even by water, and then cometh the baptism of fire and of the Holy Ghost. Behold, verily, verily, I say unto you, this is my gospel; and remember that they shall have faith in me or they can in nowise be saved.

SIT.: In this revelation given through Joseph Smith to Ezra Thayre and Northrop Sweet, the Lord is telling them what they should teach in their missionary calling. CON.: D & C 33:8-12.

( ) **3. 3 Ne. 27:20-21**

This is the commandment: Repent, all ye ends of the earth, and come unto me and be baptized in my name, that ye may be sanctified by the reception of the Holy Ghost, that ye may stand spotless before me at the last day. Verily, verily, I say unto you, this is my gospel; and ye know the things that ye must do in my church: for the works which ye have seen me do that shall ye also do.

SIT.: The resurrected Christ said these words to his disciples in the Americas. CON.: 3 Ne. 27: 13-21.

( ) **4. D & C 84:27**

[The preparatory gospel] is the gospel of repentance and of baptism, and the remission of sins, and the law of carnal commandments.

SIT.: This revelation on priesthood was given through Joseph Smith to elders of the church in 1832. CON.: D & C 84:17-28.

( ) **5. D & C 76:40-42**

This is the gospel...That he came into the world, even Jesus, to be crucified for the world, and to bear the sins of the world, and to sanctify the world, and to cleanse it from all unrighteousness; That through him all might be saved whom the Father had put into his power and made by him.

SIT.: This was revealed in a vision given to Joseph Smith and Sidney Rigdon in 1832. C.R.: 3 Ne. 27:13-17.

( ) **6. D & C 66:2**

Blessed are you for receiving mine everlasting covenant, even the fulness of my gospel, sent forth unto the children of men, that they might have life and be made partakers of the glories which are to be revealed in the last days.

SIT.: This revelation was given through Joseph Smith to William E. McLellin in 1831. C.R.: D & C 22:1-4; 45:9; 88:133; 101:39-40; 132:4,6,19, 26-27, 41-42.

( ) **7. Abra. 2:11**

[Through the priesthood] shall all the families of the earth be blessed, even with the blessings of the Gospel, which are the blessings of salvation, even of life eternal.

> *SIT.: This is a portion of the covenant made between the Lord and Abraham. CON.: Abra. 2:6-11. C.R.: Abra. 2:19; 3:14; Gen. 12:2-3; 13:14-16; 15:5-18; 17:1-22; 22:15-18.*

( ) **8. Mk. 1:15**

The time is fulfilled, and the kingdom of God is at hand: repent ye, and believe the gospel.

> *SIT.: These words were spoken by Jesus as he began his ministry by preaching in Galilee. CON.: Mk. 1:9-15.*

( ) **9. Ro. 1:16**

I am not ashamed of the gospel of Christ: for it is the power of God unto salvation to every one that believeth.

> *SIT.: Paul has written to the saints in Rome announcing that he plans to visit them to preach the gospel to them. CON.: Ro. 1:15-17.*

( ) **10. 2 Ne. 31:17**

Do the things which I have told you I have seen that your Lord and your Redeemer should do; for, for this cause have they been shown unto me, that ye might know the gate by which ye should enter. For the gate by which ye should enter is repentance and baptism by water; and then cometh a remission of your sins by fire and by the Holy Ghost.

SIT.: This counsel is written by Nephi after he has predicted the baptism of the Savior and explained its purpose.

33. FIRST PRINCIPLES OF THE GOSPEL

Faith

( ) **1. Hebrews 11:1**

Faith is the substance of things hoped for, the evidence of things not seen.

SIT.: Paul was writing to the Jews. USE: Definition of faith. C.R.: Al. 32:21; Eth. 12:6.

( ) **2. 2 Chronicles 20:20**

Believe in the LORD your God, so shall ye be established; believe his prophets, so shall ye prosper.

SIT.: Jehoshaphat, a king of the kingdom of Judah, was speaking to his people. The Moabites and Ammonites had attacked. Jehoshaphat had prayed for help. God had revealed to a prophet that he would fight the battle for them. Jehoshaphat's words were to convince his people that they should believe the revelation they had just received. CON.: 2 Chron. 20:1-29.

( ) **3. Ether 12:6**

Faith is things which are hoped for and not seen; wherefore, dispute not because ye see not, for ye receive no witness until after the trial of your faith.

SIT.: Moroni was commenting on the teachings of the prophet Ether. C.R.: Heb. 11:1; Al. 32:21.

Repentance

( ) 4. Doctrine and Covenants 58:42

He who has repented of his sins, the same is forgiven, and I, the Lord, remember them no more.

( ) 5. Doctrine and Covenants 58:43

By this ye may know if a man repenteth of his sins—behold, he will confess them and forsake them.
    SIT.: This revelation was given to a small group of the Saints as they began to settle in Jackson County, Missouri in the fall of 1831.

( ) 6. Doctrine and Covenants 66:3

Repent...of those things which are not pleasing in my sight, saith the Lord, for the Lord will show them unto you.
    SIT.: This revelation was given through Joseph Smith to William E. M'Lellin. Brother M'Lellin later became an apostle.

Baptism

( ) 7. 2 Nephi 9:23

[Christ] commandeth all men that they must repent, and be baptized in his name, having perfect faith in the Holy One of Israel, or they cannot be saved in the kingdom of God.
    SIT.: Jacob, the brother of Nephi, taught these words to his brethren after explaining the doctrines of Christ's atonement, the spirit world, the resurrection, and the final judgment.

( ) 8. Moroni 8:25

The first fruits of repentance is baptism; and baptism cometh by faith unto the fulfilling the commandments; and the fulfilling the commandments bringeth remission of sins.

> *SIT.: Moroni is quoting from a letter written by his father Mormon. USE: Note that it is the fulfilling of the commandments, rather than the act of baptism itself, which brings the remission of sins (see D & C 76:51-52; also Moro. 6:4).*

( ) 9. Alma 7:15

Show unto your God that ye are willing to repent of your sins and enter into a covenant with him to keep his commandments, and witness it unto him this day by going into the waters of baptism.

> *SIT.: Alma is preaching to the people of the land of Gideon. C.R.: Mos. 18:10, 13; 5:5; 21:35; D & C 20:37, 68-69; Moro. 6:1-4.*

Holy Ghost

( ) 10. Doctrine and Covenants 33:15

Whoso having faith you shall confirm in my church, by the laying on of the hands, and I will bestow the gift of the Holy Ghost upon them.

> *SIT.: This revelation was given through Joseph Smith to Ezra Thayre and Northrop Sweet in 1830. USE: Note that it is not the act of confirmation itself which gives the gift of the Holy Ghost; rather, the Lord promises he will give that gift to those who have been confirmed. Thus a per-*

son may be confirmed, but if he is not properly prepared the Lord may withhold the gift.

( ) **11. Doctrine and Covenants 18:18**

Ask the Father in my name, in faith believing that you shall receive, and you shall have the Holy Ghost, which manifesteth all things which are expedient unto the children of men.

SIT.: This revelation was given to Joseph Smith, Oliver Cowdery and David Whitmer in June, 1829. This promise of the Holy Ghost was thus given almost a year before the church was restored.

( ) **12. Doctrine and Covenants 11:12**

Put your trust in that Spirit which leadeth to do good—yea, to do justly, to walk humbly, to judge righteously; and this is my Spirit.

SIT.: This revelation was given through Joseph Smith to his brother, Hyrum Smith, in May, 1829.

34. FAITH

( ) **1. Prov. 3:5-6**

Trust in the LORD with all thine heart; and lean not unto thine own understanding. In all thy ways acknowledge him, and he shall direct thy paths.
CON.: Prov. 3:5-10.

( ) **2. Al. 32:21**

Faith is not to have a perfect knowledge of things; therefore if ye have faith ye hope for things which are not seen, which are true.
SIT.: Alma gave this definition of faith as he labored among the poor of the Zoramites in Antionum. CON.: Al. 32:21-43. C.R.: Heb. 11:1.

( ) **3. Ro. 10:17**

Faith cometh by hearing, and hearing by the word of God.
SIT.: Paul was explaining that men must hear about Christ if they are to believe in him. CON.: Ro. 10:8-18.

( ) **4. Eth. 12:29-30**

O Lord, thy righteous will be done, for I know that thou workest unto the children of men according to their faith; For the brother of Jared said unto the mountain Zerin, Remove—and it was removed. And if he had not had faith it would not have moved; wherefore thou workest after men have faith.
SIT.: Moroni is responding to a revelation he has

just *received from the Lord concerning faith.*
CON.: *Eth. 12:26-35. C.R.: Moses 7:13; 6:34;*
Num. 16:28-33; Mt. 17:20; Morm. 8:24; Abra. 2:7.

( ) **5. 1 Ne. 17:50**

If God had commanded me to do all things I could
do them. If he should command me that I should say
unto this water, be thou earth, it should be earth;
and if I should say it, it would be done.

SIT.: Nephi was rebuking his wicked brothers be-
cause they challenged his ability to build the
ship God had commanded him to construct. CON.:
1 Ne. 17:45-55. C.R.: Hel. 10:4-5.

( ) **6. Mt. 17:20**

If ye have faith as a grain of mustard seed, ye shall
say unto this mountain, Remove hence to yonder
place; and it shall remove; and nothing shall be impossible unto you.

SIT.: The disciples of Jesus had attempted un-
successfully to cast out an evil spirit. Jesus
made this statement to them as he explained that
their unbelief had prevented them. CON.: Mt.
17:14-21. C.R.: =Mk. 9:14-29; =Lk. 9:37-43.

( ) **7. Ps. 118:8**

It is better to trust in the LORD than to put confidence in man.
CON.: *Ps. 118:5-14.*

( ) **8. 3 Ne. 26:9-10**

If it shall so be that they shall believe these things

then shall the greater things be made manifest unto them. And if it so be that they will not believe these things, then shall the greater things be withheld from them, unto their condemnation.

SIT.: This was Mormon's comment concerning the Book of Mormon. He was commenting because the resurrected Christ had commanded that certain additional items of scripture be recorded. CON.: 3 Ne. 26:6-12.

( ) **9. Moro. 7:37**

It is by faith that miracles are wrought; and it is by faith that angels appear and minister unto men; wherefore, if these things have ceased wo be unto the children of men, for it is because of unbelief, and all is vain.

SIT.: Moroni is quoting the words of Mormon concerning faith, hope, and charity. CON.: Moro. 7:29-39.

( ) **10. Al. 30:40-41**

What evidence have ye that there is no God, or that Christ cometh not? I say unto you that ye have none, save it be your word only. But, behold, I have all things as a testimony that these things are true; and ye also have all things as a testimony unto you that they are true; and will ye deny them? Believest thou that these things are true?

SIT.: This is a portion of Alma's rebuttal to Kor-

ihor, the antichrist, who said that there would be no Christ and that no man could know of things to come. CON.: Al. 30:39-50.

See Part III, "Gifts of Faith." *Gifts of The Spirit*, pp. 113-187. These five chapters outline the gifts of faith, faith to heal others, faith to be healed, miracles, and helps and governments.

35. FAITH AND WORKS

( ) **1. Ro. 2:13**

Not the hearers of the law are just before God, but the doers of the law shall be justified.

SIT.: Paul is showing that God will render unto every man according to his deeds in the day of judgment. CON.: Ro. 2:5-16.

( ) **2. Jas. 1:22**

Be ye doers of the word, and not hearers only, deceiving your own selves.

SIT.: James is emphasizing that to hear the word accomplishes but little for it is soon forgotten; one must become involved. CON.: Jas. 1:22-27.

( ) **3. Jas. 2:20**

But wilt thou know, O vain man, that faith without works is dead?

SIT.: James is showing that man cannot be saved unless his faith is manifested through his works. CON.: Jas. 2:14-26.

( ) **4. Jas. 2:26**

As the body without the spirit is dead, so faith without works is dead also.

SIT.: James is showing that man cannot be saved unless his faith is manifested through his works. CON.: Jas. 2:14-26.

( ) **5. Morm. 9:27**

Doubt not, but be believing, and begin as in times

of old, and come unto the Lord with all your heart, and work out your own salvation with fear and trembling before him.

SIT.: Moroni gives this counsel in his Address to Unbelievers. *CON.: Morm. 9:27-28*

( ) **6. 2 Ne. 25:23**

We labor diligently to write, to persuade our children, and also our brethren, to believe in Christ, and to be reconciled to God; for we know that it is by grace that we are saved, after all we can do.

SIT.: Nephi is explaining the motive for his writing on the Book of Mormon plates. CON.: 2 Ne. 25:20-23.

( ) **7. Eph. 2:8-10**

By grace are ye saved through faith; and that not of yourselves: it is the gift of God: Not of works, lest any man should boast. For we are his workmanship, created in Christ Jesus unto good works, which God hath before ordained that we should walk in them.

NOTE: The first portion of this passage is often used to support the faith alone doctrine, yet the latter portion brings it into proper perspective. It is God's grace which saves man, yet he will not give his grace to those who do not perform good works.

( ) **8. Ro. 2:6-8**

[God] will render to every man according to his deeds: To them who by patient continuance in well doing seek for glory and honour and immortality, eternal life: But unto them that are contentious, and do not obey the truth, but obey unrighteousness, indignation and wrath.

SIT.: Paul is showing that justification is reserved for those who perform good works. CON.: Ro. 2:5-16.

( ) **9. Mt. 16:27**

The Son of man shall come in the glory of his Father with his angels; and then he shall reward every man according to his works.

SIT.: Jesus gave this teaching to Peter as he explained his impending death. CON.: Mt. 16: 21-28. C.R.: =Mk. 8:31-9:1; =Lk. 9:23-27.

( ) **10. Eth. 12:12**

If there be no faith among the children of men God can do no miracle among them; wherefore, he showeth not himself until after their faith.

SIT.: Moroni is explaining the nature of faith. CON.: Eth. 12:6-22. C.R.: Mt. 13:53-58; Jn. 1: 10-11; Mk. 6:1-6.

See "Have Faith," *Prophets and Prophecies of The Old Testament*, pp. 101-102, for an extensive listing of passages on faith.

36. REPENTANCE

( ) **1. D & C 10:67**

This is my doctrine—whosoever repenteth and cometh unto me, the same is my church.

SIT.: This revelation was given to Joseph Smith in 1828. CON.: D & C 10:67-69.

( ) **2. D & C 64:7**

I, the Lord, forgive sins unto those who confess their sins before me and ask forgiveness, who have not sinned unto death.

SIT.: This revelation was given through Joseph Smith to elders of the church in 1831. The Lord was explaining the nature of forgiveness. CON.: D & C 64:7-14.

( ) **3. D & C 63:63**

Let the church repent of their sins, and I, the Lord, will own them; otherwise they shall be cut off.

SIT.: This revelation was given through Joseph Smith to the church in 1831.

( ) **4. Mos. 26:30**

As often as my people repent will I forgive them their trespasses against me.

SIT.: The Lord spoke these words in a revelation to Alma. CON.: Mos. 26:22-32.

( ) **5. D & C 82:7**

Go your ways and sin no more; but unto that soul

who sinneth shall the former sins return, saith the Lord your God.

SIT.: This revelation was given through Joseph Smith to the church in 1832. CON.: D & C 82:1-10.

( ) **6. Al. 42:13**

According to justice, the plan of redemption could not be brought about, only on conditions of repentance of men in this probationary state.

SIT.: Alma is explaining the principles of mercy and justice to his son Corianton. CON.: Al. 42: 1-28.

( ) **7. D & C 19:15-16**

I command you to repent—repent, lest I smite you by the rod of my mouth, and by my wrath, and by my anger, and your sufferings be sore—how sore you know not, how exquisite you know not, yea, how hard to bear you know not. For behold, I, God, have suffered these things for all, that they might not suffer if they would repent.

SIT.: This commandment was revealed through Joseph Smith to Martin Harris in 1830. The Lord is explaining the nature of eternal punishment. CON.: D & C 19:13-21.

( ) **8. D & C 1:33**

He that repents not, from him shall be taken even the light which he has received; for my Spirit shall not always strive with man, saith the Lord of Hosts.

SIT.: This revelation was given through Joseph Smith to the church in 1831. CON.: D & C 1:31-35.

( ) **9. Hel. 14:13**

If ye believe on his name ye will repent of all your sins, that thereby ye may have a remission of them through his merits.

SIT.: While prophesying of the birth and death of Christ Samuel the Lamanite made this statement to the inhabitants of Zarahemla. CON.: Hel. 14: 11-13.

( ) **10. 2 Cor. 7:10**

Godly sorrow worketh repentance to salvation not to be repented of: but the sorrow of the world worketh death.

SIT.: Paul is commenting on the godly sorrow unto repentance caused by his first epistle to the Corinthians. CON.: 2 Cor. 7:8-12.

See "Repentance," *Gifts of The Spirit,* pp. 305-316; also "Repent," *Prophets and Prophecies of The Old Testament,* pp. 109-111, for an explanation of this doctrine and an extensive listing of pertinent scriptural passages.

37. BAPTISM

( ) **1. 2 Ne. 31:6**

I would ask of you, my beloved brethren, wherein the Lamb of God did fulfil all righteousness in being baptized by water?

( ) **2. 2 Ne. 31:7**

Know ye not that he was holy? But notwithstanding he being holy, he showeth unto the children of men that, according to the flesh he humbleth himself before the Father, and witnesseth unto the Father that he would be obedient unto him in keeping his commandments.

SIT.: Nephi is predicting the baptism of the Savior and explaining why he should be baptized. CON.: 2 Ne. 31:4-13.

( ) **3. 2 Ne. 31:9**

It showeth unto the children of men the straightness of the path, and the narrowness of the gate, by which they should enter, he having set the example before them.

SIT.: Nephi is predicting the baptism of the Savior and explaining why he should be baptized. CON.: 2 Ne. 31:4-13.

( ) **4. Mt. 7:13-14**

Enter ye in at the strait gate: for wide is the gate, and broad is the way, that leadeth to destruction, and many there be which go in thereat: Because strait is the gate, and narrow is the way, which leadeth unto life, and few there be that find it.

SIT.: These words were spoken by Jesus in his
Sermon on the Mount. *C.R.:* =3 *Ne.* 14:13-14; 2 *Ne.*
31:9, 17; D & C 132:22-25.

( ) **5. Ro. 6:4**

We are buried with him by baptism into death: that
like as Christ was raised up from the dead by the
glory of the Father, even so we also should walk in
newness of life.

SIT.: Paul is comparing baptism to the death and
resurrection of Christ. CON.: Ro. 6:3-13.

( ) **6. D & C 76:51-52**

They are they who received the testimony of Jesus,
and believed on his name and were baptized after
the manner of his burial, being buried in the water
in his name, and this according to the commandment
which he has given—That by keeping the commandments they might be washed and cleansed from all
their sins.

SIT.: In this vision given to Joseph Smith and
Sidney Rigdon in 1832, they were shown that bap
tism is a requirement which must be met by all
who come into the celestial kingdom. CON.:
D & C 76:50-70.

( ) **7. D & C 84:74**

They who believe not on your words, and are not
baptized in water in my name, for the remission of
their sins, that they may receive the Holy Ghost,
shall be damned, and shall not come into my Fa·

ther's kingdom where my Father and I am.

SIT.: This revelation was given through Joseph Smith to elders of the church in 1832. The Lord is speaking to those who will preach the gospel in the last days. CON.: D & C 84:61-76.

( ) **8. Jn. 3:23**

John also was baptizing in Aenon near to Salim, because there was much water there: and they came, and were baptized.

USE: This passage, like Ro. 6:3-5, is useful in showing that baptism was performed by immersion. Why would John go to a place where there was much water if he needed only to sprinkle his converts? C.R.: Mt. 3:13-17; Mk. 1:4-5.

( ) **9. Col. 2:12**

[Ye are] Buried with him in baptism, wherein also ye are risen with him through the faith of the operation of God, who hath raised him from the dead.

SIT.: Paul is exhorting the saints to walk in the ways of Christ. CON.: Col. 2:6-13.

( ) **10. Moro. 8:11**

Little children need no repentance, neither baptism. Behold, baptism is unto repentance to the fulfilling the commandments unto the remission of sins.

SIT.: Moroni is quoting the epistle of his father Mormon concerning infant baptism. CON.: Moro. 8:8-26.

38. THE BAPTISMAL COVENANT

( ) **1. Mosiah 18:10**

What have you against being baptized in the name of the Lord, as a witness before him that ye have entered into a covenant with him, that ye will serve him and keep his commandments, that he may pour out his Spirit more abundantly upon you?

SIT.: Alma was preaching to a group of people at the waters of Mormon. This was his call to them to come forward and be baptized.

( ) **2. Mosiah 18:13**

I baptize thee, having authority from the Almighty God, as a testimony that ye have entered into a covenant to serve him until you are dead as to the mortal body; and may the Spirit of the Lord be poured out upon you; and may he grant unto you eternal life, through the redemption of Christ.

SIT.: Alma used these words as he baptized Helam, the first of his converts at the waters of Mormon.

( ) **3. Mosiah 5:5**

We are willing to enter into a covenant with our God to do his will, and to be obedient to his commandments in all things that he shall command us, all the remainder of our days, that we may not bring upon ourselves a never-ending torment.

SIT.: The people had just heard a powerful address by the righteous King Benjamin. They re-

*sponded to his message by expressing their will-
ingness to enter into a covenant with God.*

( ) 4. Mosiah 21:35

They were desirous to be baptized as a witness and
a testimony that they were willing to serve God with
all their hearts.

*SIT.: This is the description given in the record
of Zeniff of the people ruled by King Limhi, to
whom Ammon had preached.*

( ) 5. Doctrine and Covenants 20:69

The members shall manifest before the church, and
also before the elders, by a godly walk and conversation, that they are worthy of it, that there may be
works and faith agreeable to the holy scriptures—
walking in holiness before the Lord.

*SIT.: This revelation was obtained by Joseph
Smith just before the church was organized in
1830. This section is one of the most important
sections of the Doctrine and Covenants, because
it gives many of the rules for the governing of
the church.*

39. PREPARATION OF NEW MEMBERS

( ) **1. D & C 20:37**

All those who humble themselves before God, and desire to be baptized, and come forth with broken hearts and contrite spirits, and witness before the church that they have truly repented of all their sins, and are willing to take upon them the name of Jesus Christ, having a determination to serve him to the end, and truly manifest by their works that they have received of the Spirit of Christ unto the remission of their sins, shall be received by baptism into his church.

SIT.: This revelation was given through Joseph Smith just prior to the organization of the church in 1830.

( ) **2. D & C 20:68**

The elders or priests are to have a sufficient time to expound all things concerning the church of Christ to their understanding, previous to their partaking of the sacrament and being confirmed by the laying on of the hands of the elders, so that all things may be done in order.

SIT.: This revelation was given through Joseph Smith just prior to the organization of the church in 1830. CON.: D & C 20:68-69.

( ) **3. D & C 42:78**

Every person who belongeth to this church of Christ, shall observe to keep all the commandments and covenants of the church.

SIT.: In this revelation, given through Joseph Smith to elders of the church in 1831, the Lord is revealing the law of his church.

( ) 4. Moro. 6:1-3

They were not baptized save they brought forth fruit meet that they were worthy of it. Neither did they receive any unto baptism save they came forth with a broken heart and a contrite spirit, and witnessed unto the church that they truly repented of all their sins. And none were received unto baptism save they took upon them the name of Christ, having a determination to serve him to the end.

( ) 5. Moro. 6:4

And after they had been received unto baptism, and were wrought upon and cleansed by the power of the Holy Ghost, they were numbered among the people of the church of Christ; and their names were taken, that they might be remembered and nourished by the good word of God, to keep them in the right way, to keep them continually watchful unto prayer, relying alone upon the merits of Christ.

( ) 6. Moro. 6:5-6

And the church did meet together oft, to fast and to pray, and to speak one with another concerning the welfare of their souls. And they did meet together oft to partake of bread and wine, in remembrance of the Lord Jesus.

SIT.: Moroni is discussing the preparation and treatment of those received into the church in his day. CON.: Moro. 6:1-9.

( ) **7. Mos. 18:8**

Ye are desirous to come into the fold of God, and to be called his people, and are willing to bear one another's burdens, that they may be light;

( ) **8. Mos. 18:9**

Yea, and are willing to mourn with those that mourn; yea, and comfort those that stand in need of comfort, and to stand as witnesses of God at all times and in all things, and in all places that ye may be in, even until death, that ye may be redeemed of God, and be numbered with those of the first resurrection, that ye may have eternal life.

> *SIT.: Alma gave this description of those whom he was about to baptize as he met with them at the waters of Mormon. CON.: Mos. 18:8-29.*

( ) **9. Mos. 18:21-22**

He commanded them that there should be no contention one with another, but that they should look forward with one eye, having one faith and one baptism, having their hearts knit together in unity and in love one towards another. And thus he commanded them to preach. And thus they became the children of God.

> *SIT.: Alma gave these commandments to the members he had just baptized at the waters of Mormon. CON.: Mos. 18:8-29.*

( ) **10. 3 Ne. 27:7**

Whatsoever ye shall do, ye shall do it in my name; therefore ye shall call the church in my name; and ye shall call upon the Father in my name that he will bless the church for my sake.

SIT.: Jesus appeared to his disciples in the Americas and gave them this counsel in response to their plea for more information concerning his church. CON.: 3 Ne. 27:1-12.

40. LEARN YOUR DUTY

( ) 1. D & C 107:99-100

Let every man learn his duty, and to act in the office
in which he is appointed, in all diligence. He that
is slothful shall not be counted worthy to stand,
and he that learns not his duty and shows himself
not approved shall not be counted worthy to stand.

*SIT.: In this revelation, which was given through
Joseph Smith to the church in 1835, the Lord
revealed the duties of priesthood officials.*

( ) 2. D & C 53:1

I have heard your prayers; and you have called upon
me that it should be made known unto you, of the
Lord your God, concerning your calling and election
in the church, which I, the Lord, have raised up in
these last days.

*SIT.: This revelation was given through Joseph
Smith to Sidney Gilbert in 1831.*

( ) 3. Eccles. 12:13

Let us hear the conclusion of the whole matter:
Fear God, and keep his commandments: for this is
the whole duty of man.

*SIT.: This is the end of the book of Ecclesiastes,
which tells of the preacher's search to find what
will bring happiness to man.*

( ) 4. D & C 105:9-10

In consequence of the transgressions of my people,

it is expedient in me that mine elders should wait
for a little season for the redemption of Zion—That
they themselves may be prepared, and that my
people may be taught more perfectly, and have experience, and know more perfectly concerning their
duty, and the things which I require at their hands.

*SIT.: In this revelation, which was given through
Joseph Smith to the church in 1834, the Lord
reveals that the saints must reach a greater degree of perfection before the New Jerusalem can
be established. CON.: D & C 105:1-17.*

( ) **5. D & C 43:8**

I give unto you a commandment, that when ye are
assembled together ye shall instruct and edify each
other, that ye may know how to act and direct my
church, how to act upon the points of my law and
commandments, which I have given.

*SIT.: In this revelation, which was given through
Joseph Smith to the church in 1831, the Lord
gives guidelines to the saints so that they might
know how revelations are to be received and
taught in the church. CON.: D & C 43:1-16.*

( ) **6. JS 2:46**

This he forbade me, saying that I must have no other
object in view in getting the plates but to glorify
God, and must not be influenced by any other motive
than that of building his kingdom; otherwise I could
not get them.

*SIT.: Joseph Smith is telling the message given
in Moroni's third appearance to him, when he was*

warned that Satan would try to tempt him to get the plates for the purpose of getting rich.

( ) 7. **D & C 23:3**

Thy calling is to exhortation, and to strengthen the church continually. Wherefore thy duty is unto the church forever, and this because of thy family.

SIT.: This revelation was given through Joseph Smith to his brother, Hyrum Smith, in 1830.

( ) 8. **D & C 23:7**

It is your duty to unite with the true church, and give your language to exhortation continually, that you may receive the reward of the laborer.

SIT.: This revelation was given through Joseph Smith to Joseph Knight, Sr., in 1830.

( ) 9. **D & C 64:29**

Wherefore, as ye are agents, ye are on the Lord's errand; and whatever ye do according to the will of the Lord is the Lord's business.

SIT.: This revelation was given through Joseph Smith to elders of the church in 1831.

( ) 10. **1 Jn. 2:27**

The anointed which ye have received of him abideth in you, and ye need not that any man teach you: but as the same anointing teacheth you of all things, and is truth, and is no lie, and even as it hath taught you, ye shall abide in him.

SIT.: John, while warning of antichrists who are preaching false doctrines, says that members can learn the things they should know through personal revelation. CON.: 1 Jn. 2:18-29.

41. FIND YOUR CALLING

( ) **1. D & C 81:4**

In doing these things thou wilt do the greatest good unto thy fellow beings, and wilt promote the glory of him who is your Lord.

SIT.: This revelation was given through Joseph Smith to Frederick G. Williams in 1832. The Lord here stresses the objectives man must seek to fulfill as he labors throughout mortality.

( ) **2. Ro. 6:13**

Neither yield ye your members as instruments of unrighteousness unto sin: but yield yourselves unto God, as those that are alive from the dead, and your members as instruments of righteousness unto God.

SIT.:Paul is showing that those who are baptized must be dead to sin. CON.: Ro. 6:1-14.

( ) **3. D & C 103:9**

They were set to be a light unto the world, and to be the saviors of men.

SIT.: This revelation was given through Joseph Smith to the church in 1834. The Lord is speaking of the destiny of the saints. CON.: D & C 103:5-10

( ) **4. D & C 15:6**

The thing which will be of the most worth unto you will be to declare repentance unto this people, that you may bring souls unto me, that you may rest with them in the kingdom of my Father.

SIT.: This revelation was given through Joseph Smith to John Whitmer in 1829, in response to inquiry as to what should be his individual duty and calling. C.R.: =D & C 16:6.

( ) **5. D & C 90:16**

This shall be your business and mission in all your lives, to preside in council, and set in order all the affairs of this church and kingdom.

SIT.: This revelation was given to Joseph Smith in 1833. CON.: D & C 90:12-18.

( ) **6. Ro. 8:28**

All things work together for good to them that love God, to them who are the called according to his purpose.

SIT.: Paul is speaking of the blessings available to the saints because they are the elect of God. CON.: Ro. 8:28-33.

( ) **7. 1 Ne. 21:4**

Surely my judgment is with the Lord, and my work with my God.

SIT.: Nephi is quoting from the writings of Isaiah, as found on the plates of brass. Isaiah is setting forth a "Servant Song," in which he is prophesying of the mortal mission of the Savior. CON.: 1 Ne. 21:1-6.

( ) **8. Ezra 7:10**

Ezra had prepared his heart to seek the law of the
LORD, and to do it, and to teach in Israel statutes
and judgments.

*SIT.: This is a description of Ezra the scribe,
who led a group of the people of Judah out of
Babylon back to their promised land.*

( ) **9. D & C 58:1**

Hearken, O ye elders of my church, and give ear to
my word, and learn of me what I will concerning you,
and also concerning this land unto which I have
sent you.

*SIT.: This revelation was given through Joseph
Smith to the church in 1831. CON.: D & C 58:1-5.*

( ) **10. D & C 24:7**

Thou shalt devote all thy service in Zion; and in
this thou shalt have strength.

*SIT.: This revelation was given to Joseph Smith
and Oliver Cowdery in 1830. In this portion the
Lord is speaking to Joseph Smith. CON.: D & C
24:1-9.*

42. LABOR WITH ALL YOUR MIGHT

( ) **1. Jac. 1:19**

We did magnify our office unto the Lord, taking upon
us the responsibility, answering the sins of the people upon our own heads if we did not teach them the
word of God with all diligence; wherefore, by labor-
ing with our might their blood might not come upon
our garments; otherwise their blood would come upon
our garments, and we would not be found spotless
at the last day.

*SIT.: Jacob is telling of the labors which he and
his brother Joseph performed. CON.: Jac. 1:17-19.
C.R.: Ezek. 33:1-9.*

( ) **2. D & C 38:40**

I give unto you a commandment, that every man, both
elder, priest, teacher, and also member, go to with
his might, with the labor of his hands, to prepare
and accomplish the things which I have commanded.

*SIT.: This commandment was given through Jo-
seph Smith to the church in 1831. CON.: D & C
38:40-42.*

( ) **3. D & C 58:29**

He that doeth not anything until he is commanded,
and receiveth a commandment with doubtful heart,
and keepeth it with slothfulness, the same is damned.

*SIT.: This revelation was given through Joseph
Smith to the church in 1831. CON.: D & C 58:
26-33.*

( ) **4. Gal. 6:9-10**

Let us not be weary in well doing: for in due season we shall reap, if we faint not. As we have therefore opportunity, let us do good unto all men, especially unto them who are of the household of faith.

SIT.: Paul is teaching that man will reap the reward for that which he sows. CON.: Gal. 6:7-10.

( ) **5. 1 Cor. 3:8-9**

Every man shall receive his own reward according to his own labour. For we are labourers together with God: ye are God's husbandry, ye are God's building.

SIT.: Paul rebukes the saints for being divided into factions, saying that it is not they, but God, who gives the increase in their work. CON.: 1 Cor. 3:3-15.

( ) **6. 2 Ne. 31:20**

Ye must press forward with a steadfastness in Christ, having a perfect brightness of hope, and a love of God and of all men. Wherefore, if ye shall press forward, feasting upon the word of Christ, and endure to the end, behold, thus saith the Father: Ye shall have eternal life.

SIT.: Nephi concludes his explanation of the baptism of Christ with this exhortation. CON.: 2 Ne. 31:15-21.

( ) **7. 2 Cor. 9:6**

He which soweth sparingly shall reap also sparingly; and he which soweth bountifully shall reap also bountifully.

SIT.: Paul is commending the saints in Corinth for their zeal in preparing contributions for the poor among the saints. CON.: 2 Cor. 9:1-9.

( ) **8. 1 Cor. 9:24**

Know ye not that they which run in a race run all, but one receiveth the prize? So run, that ye may obtain.

SIT.: Paul is showing that every man must strive to gain his eternal crown. CON.: 1 Cor. 9:24-27.

( ) **9. D & C 54:9**

Seek ye a living like unto men, until I prepare a place for you.

SIT.: This revelation was given through Joseph Smith to Newel Knight in 1831.

( ) **10. Mos. 4:27**

See that all these things are done in wisdom and order; for it is not requisite that a man should run faster than he has strength. And again, it is expedient that he should be diligent, that thereby he might win the prize; therefore, all things must be done in order.

SIT.: King Benjamin is teaching his people that they should care for the poor and needy. CON.: Mos. 4:22-28. C.R.: D & C 10:4.

43. MAGNIFY THE PRIESTHOOD

( ) 1. 1 Pet. 2:9

Ye are a chosen generation, a royal priesthood, an holy nation, a peculiar people; that ye should shew forth the praises of him who hath called you out of darkness into his marvellous light.

SIT.: Peter is telling the saints that they, as the priesthood, are to offer up spiritual sacrifices unto God. CON.: 1 Pet. 2:1-10.

( ) 2. D & C 50:13-14

I the Lord ask you this question—unto what were ye ordained? To preach my gospel by the Spirit, even the Comforter which was sent forth to teach the truth.

SIT.: In this revelation, which was given through Joseph Smith to elders of the church in 1831, the Lord reasons with the elders concerning their use of the priesthood. CON.: D & C 50:10-20.

( ) 3. Al. 43:2

They preached the word, and the truth, according to the spirit of prophecy and revelation; and they preached after the holy order of God by which they were called.

SIT.: This is a description of the preaching of Alma and his sons.

( ) 4. D & C 46:2

Notwithstanding those things which are written, it always has been given to the elders of my church from the beginning, and ever shall be, to conduct all meetings as they are directed and guided by the Holy Spirit.

SIT.: This revelation was given through Joseph Smith to the church in 1831. The revelation deals with the Spirit and spiritual gifts. CON.: D & C 46:1-6.

( ) 5. **2 Ne. 32:9**

Ye must not perform any thing unto the Lord save in the first place ye shall pray unto the Father in the name of Christ, that he will consecrate thy performance unto thee, that thy performance may be for the welfare of thy soul.

SIT.: Nephi is teaching that if one is to work by the Spirit he must pray for guidance. CON.: 2 Ne. 32:7-9.

( ) 6. **D & C 121:39-40**

We have learned by sad experience that it is the nature and disposition of almost all men, as soon as they get a little authority, as they suppose, they will immediately begin to exercise unrighteous dominion. Hence many are called, but few are chosen.

( ) 7. **D & C 121:41-42**

No power or influence can or ought to be maintained by virtue of the priesthood, only by persuasion, by long-suffering, by gentleness and meekness, and by love unfeigned; By kindness, and pure knowledge, which shall greatly enlarge the soul without hypocrisy, and without guile—

( ) 8. D & C 121:43-44

Reproving betimes with sharpness, when moved upon by the Holy Ghost; and then showing forth afterwards an increase of love toward him whom thou hast reproved, lest he esteem thee to be his enemy; That he may know that thy faithfulness is stronger than the cords of death.

SIT.: This revelation was given to Joseph Smith in 1839. The Lord is explaining how men should use the priesthood power which is given to them.

( ) 9. D & C 84:109-110

Let every man stand in his own office, and labor in his own calling; and let not the head say unto the feet it hath no need of the feet; for without the feet how shall the body be able to stand? Also the body hath need of every member, that all may be edified together, that the system may be kept perfect.

SIT.: In this revelation, which was given through Joseph Smith to elders of the church in 1832, the Lord gives extensive instruction concerning the priesthood. CON.: D & C 84:106-112. C.R.: 1 Cor. 12:13-29.

( ) 10. 1 Tim. 5:17

Let the elders that rule well be counted worthy of double honour, especially they who labour in the word and doctrine.

SIT.: Paul is giving instruction concerning respect for elders and widows in the church. CON.: 1 Tim. 5:17-20.

44. GAIN PRIESTHOOD POWER

( ) 1. Jac. 4:6

We search the prophets, and we have many revelations and the spirit of prophecy; and having all these witnesses we obtain a hope, and our faith becometh unshaken, insomuch that we truly can command in the name of Jesus and the very trees obey us, or the mountains, or the waves of the sea.

SIT.: Jacob is telling of his labors in the ministry. CON.: Jac. 4:6-10.

( ) 2. Hel. 10:4

Blessed art thou, Nephi, for those things which thou hast done; for I have beheld how thou hast with unwearyingness declared the word, which I have given unto thee, unto this people. And thou hast not feared them, and hast not sought thine own life, but hast sought my will, and to keep my commandments.

( ) 3. Hel. 10:5

And now, because thou hast done this with such unwearyingness, behold, I will bless thee forever; and I will make thee mighty in word and in deed, in faith and in works; yea, even that all things shall be done unto thee according to thy word, for thou shalt not ask that which is contrary to my will.

SIT.: As Nephi was pondering the great wickedness of his people, a voice spoke to him and gave him this great promise of power. CON.: Hel. 10:3-11.

( ) 4. **D & C 121:45**

Let thy bowels also be full of charity towards all men, and to the household of faith, and let virtue garnish thy thoughts unceasingly; then shall thy confidence wax strong in the presence of God; and the doctrine of the priesthood shall distil upon thy soul as the dews from heaven.

( ) 5. **D & C 121:46**

The Holy Ghost shall be thy constant companion, and thy scepter an unchanging scepter of righteousness and truth; and thy dominion shall be an everlasting dominion, and without compulsory means it shall flow unto thee forever and ever.

SIT.: This revelation was given to Joseph Smith in 1839. The Lord is explaining how men should use the priesthood power which is given to them.

( ) 6. **D & C 50:35**

The kingdom is given you of the Father, and power to overcome all things which are not ordained of him.

SIT.: This revelation was given through Joseph Smith to elders of the church in 1831.

( ) 7. **D & C 71:6**

Unto him that receiveth it shall be given more abundantly, even power.

SIT.: This revelation was given to Joseph Smith and Sidney Rigdon in 1831. CON.: D & C 71:4-10.

( ) 8. **1 Ne. 17:48**

In the name of the Almighty God, I command you that

ye touch me not, for I am filled with the power of God, even unto the consuming of my flesh; and who-so shall lay his hands upon me shall wither even as a dried reed; and he shall be as naught before the power of God, for God shall smite him.

SIT.: Nephi said these words as he rebuked his brothers for their attempt to kill him. CON.: 1 Ne. 17:45-54. C.R.: Mos. 13:3-5.

( ) **9. Moses 6:34**

My Spirit is upon you, wherefore all thy words will I justify; and the mountains shall flee before you, and the rivers shall turn from their course; and thou shalt abide in me, and I in you; therefore walk with me.

SIT.: The Lord made this promise to Enoch. CON.: Moses 6:31-34. C.R.: Moses 7:13.

( ) **10. D & C 84:106**

If any man among you be strong in the Spirit, let him take with him him that is weak, that he may be edified in all meekness, that he may become strong also.

SIT.: In this revelation, which was given through Joseph Smith to elders of the church in 1832, the Lord gives extensive instruction concerning the priesthood. CON.: D & C 84:106-112.

45. BRING TO PASS RIGHTEOUSNESS

( ) 1. **Mt. 7:16-18**

Ye shall know them by their fruits. Do men gather grapes of thorns, or figs of thistles? Even so every good tree bringeth forth good fruit; but a corrupt tree bringeth forth evil fruit. A good tree cannot bring forth evil fruit, neither can a corrupt tree bring forth good fruit.

SIT.: Jesus gave this counsel in his Sermon on the Mount. *CON.: Mt. 7:15-23. C.R.: Lk. 6:43-45; =3 Ne. 14:15-23.*

( ) 2. **Moro. 7:13-14**

That which is of God inviteth and enticeth to do good continually; wherefore, every thing which inviteth and enticeth to do good, and to love God, and to serve him, is inspired of God. Wherefore, take heed, my beloved brethren, that ye do not judge that which is evil to be of God, or that which is good and of God to be of the devil.

SIT.: Moroni is citing the teachings of his father, Mormon, about things which entice men to do either good or evil. CON.: Moro. 7:5-19.

( ) 3. **D & C 6:8**

As you desire of me so it shall be unto you; and if you desire, you shall be the means of doing much good in this generation.

SIT.: This revelation was given to Joseph Smith and Oliver Cowdery in 1829. CON.: D & C 6:5-8.

( ) **4. 2 Thess. 3:13**

Brethren, be not weary in well doing.

SIT.: Paul is telling the saints that they must all work and support themselves. CON.: 2 Thess. 3:10-14.

( ) **5. D & C 59:23**

Learn that he who doeth the works of righteousness shall receive his reward, even peace in this world, and eternal life in the world to come.

SIT.: This revelation was given through Joseph Smith to the church in 1831. The Lord is speaking of those who keep his commandments. CON.: D & C 59:21-24.

( ) **6. 2 Cor. 8:3**

To their power, I bear record, yea, and beyond their power they were willing of themselves.

SIT.: Paul is speaking of the great liberality manifested by the saints in Macedonia in contributing to the poor of the church. CON.: 2 Cor. 8:1-5.

( ) **7. D & C 6:33**

Fear not to do good, my sons, for whatsoever ye sow, that shall ye also reap; therefore, if ye sow good ye shall also reap good for your reward.

SIT.: This revelation was given to Joseph Smith and Oliver Cowdery in 1829. CON.: D & C 6: 27-35.

( ) **8. 2 Tim. 2:15**

Study to shew thyself approved unto God, a workman

that needeth not to be ashamed, rightly dividing the word of truth.

SIT.: Paul is telling Timothy to study to learn the truth, but to avoid false doctrines. CON.: 2 Tim. 2:14-19.

( ) **9. D & C 58:26**

It is not meet that I should command in all things; for he that is compelled in all things, the same is a slothful and not a wise servant; wherefore he receiveth no reward.

SIT.: In this revelation, which was given through Joseph Smith to elders of the church in 1831, the Lord instructs the saints that they must be willing to initiate works of righteousness without having to be commanded. CON.: D & C 58:26-33.

( ) **10. 1 Cor. 15:58**

Be ye steadfast, unmoveable, always abounding in the work of the Lord, forasmuch as ye know that your labour is not in vain in the Lord.

SIT.: Paul concludes his explanation of the doctrine of the resurrection with these words.

46. BE AN EXAMPLE

( ) 1. 1 Tim. 4:12

Be thou an example of the believers, in word, in conversation, in charity, in spirit, in faith, in purity.
  SIT.: Paul is giving counsel to Timothy to aid him in his ministry. CON.: 1 Tim. 4:6-16.

( ) 2. Mt. 5:16

Let your light so shine before men, that they may see your good works, and glorify your Father which is in heaven.
  SIT.: Jesus gave this counsel in his Sermon on the Mount. CON.: Mt. 5:13-16. C.R.: = 3 Ne. 12:13-16.

( ) 3. D & C 108:7

Strengthen your brethren in all your conversation, in all your prayers, in all your exhortations, and in all your doings.
  SIT.: This revelation was given through Joseph Smith to Lyman Sherman in 1835.

( ) 4. Jac. 2:35

Ye have broken the hearts of your tender wives, and lost the confidence of your children, because of your bad examples before them; and the sobbings of their hearts ascend up to God against you. And because of the strictness of the word of God, which cometh down against you, many hearts died, pierced with deep wounds.

SIT.: Jacob is denouncing the Nephites because of their unchastity. CON.: Jac. 2:23-35.

( ) **5. Jac. 3:10**

Ye shall remember your children, how that ye have grieved their hearts because of the example that ye have set before them; and also, remember that ye may, because of your filthiness, bring your children unto destruction, and their sins be heaped upon your heads at the last day.

SIT.: Jacob is warning the Nephites of the sufferings of hell which await them because of their unchastity. CON.: Jac. 3:10-12.

( ) **6. 1 Pet. 5:2-3**

Feed the flock of God which is among you, taking the oversight thereof, not by constraint, but willingly; not for filthy lucre, but of a ready mind; Neither as being lords over God's heritage, but being ensamples to the flock.

SIT.: Paul is giving instruction to the elders of the church. CON.: 1 Pet. 5:1-5.

( ) **7. Tit. 2:7-8**

Live] In all things shewing thyself a pattern of good works: in doctrine shewing uncorruptness, gravity, sincerity, Sound speech, that cannot be condemned; that he that is of the contrary part may be ashamed, having no evil thing to say of you.

SIT.: Paul is instructing Titus how to conduct his ministry. CON.: Tit. 2:1-15.

( ) **8. Al. 39:11**

When they saw your conduct they would not believe in my words.

> *SIT.: Alma is rebuking his son Corianton for his misconduct among the Zoramites. CON.: Al. 39:2-11.*

( ) **9. Heb. 10:24-25**

Let us consider one another to provoke unto love and to good works: Not forsaking the assembling of ourselves together, as the manner of some is; but exhorting one another.

> *SIT.: Paul is exhorting the saints to hold fast to the faith. CON.: Heb. 10:22-27.*

( ) **10. D & C 115:5**

I say unto you all: Arise and shine forth, that thy light may be a standard for the nations.

> *SIT.: In this revelation, which was given through Joseph Smith to the church in 1838, the Lord gave this commandment as he revealed the name of the church. CON.: D & C 115:4-6.*

47. DEVELOP TALENTS

( ) **1. 1 Cor. 14:12**

Forasmuch as ye are zealous of spiritual gifts, seek that ye may excel to the edifying of the church.

SIT.: Paul is stressing that the members should use their gifts for the edification of others. CON.: 1 Cor. 14:12-17.

( ) **2. D & C 82:3**

Of him unto whom much is given much is required; and he who sins against the greater light shall receive the greater condemnation.

SIT.: In this revelation, which was given through Joseph Smith to the church in 1832, the Lord is warning of the consequences of sin. CON.: D & C 82:1-10. C.R.: Lk. 12:48.

( ) **3. D & C 82:18**

All this for the benefit of the church of the living God, that every man may improve upon his talent, that every man may gain other talents, yea, even an hundred fold, to be cast into the Lord's storehouse, to become the common property of the whole church.

SIT.: In this revelation, which was given through Joseph Smith to the church in 1832, the Lord is speaking of each man's responsibility in the United Order. CON.: D & C 82:14-21.

( ) **4. D & C 60:2-3**

With some I am not well pleased, for they will not

open their mouths, but they hide the talent which I have given unto them, because of the fear of man. Wo unto such, for mine anger is kindled against them. And it shall come to pass, if they are not more faithful unto me, it shall be taken away, even that which they have.

SIT.: In this revelation, which was given through Joseph Smith to elders of the church in 1831, the Lord speaks his displeasure against missionaries who are reluctant to preach his gospel.   C.R.: Mt. 25:28-29; D & C 60:13.

( ) 5. Mt. 25:28-29

Take therefore the talent from him, and give it unto him which hath ten talents. For unto every one that hath shall be given, and he shall have abundance: but from him that hath not shall be taken away even that which he hath.

SIT.: Jesus, while telling the parable of the talents, said this about the servant who buried his talent and refused to increase it.   CON.: Mt. 25:14-30.

( ) 6. 2 Cor. 8:12

If there be first a willing mind, it is accepted according to that a man hath, and not according to that he hath not.

SIT.: Paul is exhorting the saints to progress in their collections, saying they should be forward of the year previous.   CON.: 2 Cor. 8:10-15.

137

( ) **7. D & C 25:12**

My soul delighteth in the song of the heart; yea, the
song of the righteous is a prayer unto me, and it
shall be answered with a blessing upon their heads.

*SIT.: This revelation was given through Joseph
Smith to his wife, Emma Smith, in 1830.*

( ) **8. 1 Cor. 14:26**

When ye come together, every one of you hath a
psalm, hath a doctrine, hath a tongue, hath a revelation, hath an interpretation. Let all things be done
unto edifying.

*SIT.: Paul is counseling the saints to use their
talents and gifts for the edification of all the
members of the church.   CON.: 1 Cor. 14:12-33.*

( ) **9. Col. 3:16**

Let the word of Christ dwell in you richly in all
wisdom; teaching and admonishing one another in
psalms and hymns and spiritual songs, singing with
grace in your hearts to the Lord.

*SIT.: Paul is describing the actions of those who
have put on the new man in Christ.   CON.: Col.
3:9-17.*

( ) **10. Eph. 5:19**

Speaking to yourselves in psalms and hymns and
spiritual songs, singing and making melody in your
heart to the Lord.

*SIT.: Paul is describing the conduct which should
exemplify true followers of Christ.   CON.: Eph.
5:1-20.*

48. SUBMIT TO THE WILL OF GOD

( ) **1. D & C 109:44**

Thy word must be fulfilled. Help thy servants to say, with thy grace assisting them: Thy will be done, O Lord, and not ours.

SIT.: These words are from the inspired prayer revealed to Joseph Smith for use in dedicating the Kirtland temple in 1836.

( ) **2. Gal. 1:10**

Do I now persuade men, or God? or do I seek to please men? for if I yet pleased men, I should not be the servant of Christ.

SIT.: Paul makes this statement as he warns of another, false gospel which is being preached among the saints. CON.: Gal. 1:6-12.

( ) **3. 1 Cor. 1:31**

He that glorieth, let him glory in the Lord.

SIT.: Paul makes this statement as he shows that God has chosen the foolish things of the world to confound the wise. CON.: 1 Cor. 1:25-31. C.R.: Jer. 9:23-24.

( ) **4. Eph. 5:17**

Be ye not unwise, but understanding what the will of the Lord is.

SIT.: Paul is warning against following false doctrine and is instructing the saints to prove what is acceptable to the Lord. CON.: Eph. 5:6-17.

( ) 5. Col. 1:9

[We] do not cease to pray for you, and to desire that ye might be filled with the knowledge of his will in all wisdom and spiritual understanding.

SIT.: Paul is expressing his desire that the saints be worthy of the Lord. CON.: Col. 1:3-13.

( ) 6. D & C 101:42

He that exalteth himself shall be abased, and he that abaseth himself shall be exalted.

SIT.: This revelation was given to Joseph Smith in 1833. The Lord is admonishing man to care for the soul rather than the body. CON.: D & C 101:36-42.

( ) 7. 2 Ne. 26:29

He commandeth that there shall be no priestcrafts; for, behold, priestcrafts are that men preach and set themselves up for a light unto the world, that they may get gain and praise of the world; but they seek not the welfare of Zion.

SIT.: Nephi makes this statement as he warns of secret combinations which he prophesies will exist in the last days. CON.: 2 Ne. 26:22-31.

( ) 8. Jn. 4:34

My most is to do the will of him that sent me, and to finish his work.

SIT.: After making the trip to Samaria, Jesus was invited by his disciples to stop and eat. He told them that he had meat to eat which they knew not of, and then gave this explanation of what that meat was. CON.: Jn. 4:31-38.

( ) 9. Lk. 22:42-43

Father, if thou be willing, remove this cup from me: nevertheless not my will, but thine, be done. And there appeared an angel unto him from heaven, strengthening him.

SIT.: Jesus offered this prayer as he suffered in the Garden of Gethsemane, just before his betrayal and arrest. CON.: Lk. 22:39-46. C.R.: =Mt. 26:36-46; =Mk. 14:32-42.

( ) 10. Ro. 2:29

[God's covenant with man] is that of the heart, in the spirit, and not in the letter; whose praise is not of men, but of God.

SIT.: Paul is speaking of God's impartial attitude toward both Jews and Gentiles. He characterizes the Jews as those who have received circumcision, which is symbolic of the covenant with God made by Abraham. See Gen. 17:1-14. CON.: Ro. 2:25-29.

49. BE HUMBLE

( ) 1. D & C 112:10

Be thou humble; and the Lord thy God shall lead
thee by the hand, and give thee answer to thy prayers.
*SIT.: This revelation was given through Joseph
Smith to Thomas B. Marsh in 1837.*

( ) 2. D & C 136:32-33

Let him that is ignorant learn wisdom by humbling
himself and calling upon the Lord his God, that his
eyes may be opened that he may see, and his ears
opened that he may hear; For my Spirit is sent forth
into the world to enlighten the humble and contrite,
and to the condemnation of the ungodly.
*SIT.: This revelation was given through Brigham
Young in 1847.*

( ) 3. 1 Cor. 3:18-19

Let no man deceive himself. If any man among you
seemeth to be wise in this world, let him become a
fool, that he may be wise. For the wisdom of this
world is foolishness with God. For it is written, He
taketh the wise in their own craftiness.
*SIT.: Paul is stressing the need for humility
among those who have built upon the foundation
of Christ. CON.: 1 Cor. 3:9-21.*

( ) 4. 1 Cor. 1:26-27

Ye see your calling, brethren, how that not many
wise men after the flesh, not many mighty, not many

noble, are called: But God hath chosen the foolish things of the world to confound the wise; and God hath chosen the weak things of the world to confound the things which are mighty.

SIT.: Paul is explaining that even the foolishness of God is wiser than the wisdom of men. CON.: 1 Cor. 1:25-31.

( ) **5. Gal. 5:25-26**

If we live in the Spirit, let us also walk in the Spirit. Let us not be desirous of vain glory, provoking one another, envying one another.

SIT.: Paul is contrasting the works of those who walk in the Spirit with the deeds of those who walk in the flesh. CON.: Gal. 5:13-26.

( ) **6. Jas. 4:9-10**

Be afflicted, and mourn, and weep: let your laughter be turned to mourning, and your joy to heaviness. Humble yourselves in the sight of the Lord, and he shall lift you up.

SIT.: James is teaching that God resists the proud but gives grace to those who are humble. CON.: Jas. 4:6-11.

( ) **7. Phil. 4:12-13**

I know both how to be abased, and I know how to abound: every where and in all things I am instructed both to be full and to be hungry, both to abound and to suffer need. I can do all things through Christ which strengtheneth me.

SIT.: Paul is expressing his gratitude that the saints in Philippi aided him in taking care of his physical needs. CON.: Phil. 4:9-19.

( ) **8. Phil. 2:3-4**

Let nothing be done through strife or vainglory; but in lowliness of mind let each esteem other better than themselves. Look not every man on his own things, but every man also on the things of others.

SIT.: Paul is exhorting the saints to follow the example of humility set by Jesus. CON.: Phil. 2:3-8.

( ) **9. D & C 52:15-16**

He that prayeth, whose spirit is contrite, the same is accepted of me if he obey mine ordinances. He that speaketh, whose spirit is contrite, whose language is meek and edifieth, the same is of God if he obey mine ordinances.

SIT.: In this revelation, which was given through Joseph Smith to elders of the church in 1831, the Lord gives this passage as a pattern whereby they might be able to discern between good and evil.

( ) **10. D & C 67:10**

Inasmuch as you strip yourselves from jealousies and fears, and humble yourselves before me, for ye are not sufficiently humble, the veil shall be rent and you shall see me and know that I am—not with the carnal neither natural mind, but with the spiritual.

SIT.: In this revelation, which was given through Joseph Smith to the church in 1831, the Lord gives this promise to those who have been ordained. CON.: D & C 67:10-14.

50. ACCEPT CHASTENING AND CORRECTION

( ) **1. Heb. 12:6-7**

Whom the Lord loveth he chasteneth, and scourgeth
every son whom he receiveth. If ye endure chastening, God dealeth with you as with sons; for what
son is he whom the father chasteneth not?

*SIT.: Paul is showing that the saints must be
willing to accept chastening so that they can be
partakers of the Lord's holiness. CON.: Heb.
12:4-11. C.R.: Prov. 3:11-12.*

( ) **2. Job 5:17-18**

Happy is the man whom God correcteth: therefore
despise not thou the chastening of the Almighty:
For he maketh sore, and bindeth up: he woundeth,
and his hands make whole.

*SIT.: Eliphaz, a friend of Job's, gives this as
the reason why Job is suffering his great afflictions. CON.: Job 5:17-27.*

( ) **3. D & C 58:3-4**

Ye cannot behold with your natural eyes, for the
present time, the design of your God concerning
those things which shall come hereafter, and the
glory which shall follow after much tribulation. For
after much tribulation come the blessings. Wherefore
the day cometh that ye shall be crowned with much
glory; the hour is not yet, but is nigh at hand.

*SIT.: This revelation was given through Joseph
Smith to elders of the church in 1831. The Lord*

is revealing his will concerning the inhabitants of Jackson Co., Mo. CON.: D & C 58:1-5.

( ) **4. D & C 136:31**

My people must be tried in all things, that they may be prepared to receive the glory that I have for them, even the glory of Zion; and he that will not bear chastisement is not worthy of my kingdom.

SIT.: This revelation was given through Brigham Young to the church in 1847.

( ) **5. Hel. 12:3**

Except the Lord doth chasten his people with many afflictions, yea, except he doth visit them with death and with terror, and with famine and with all manner of pestilence, they will not remember him.

SIT.: Nephi is commenting on the cycle which carries men from righteousness to wickedness to repentance to righteousness as they misuse the blessings of God and suffer his rebuke. CON.: Hel. 12:1-4.

( ) **6. D & C 105:6**

My people must needs be chastened until they learn obedience, if it must needs be, by the things which they suffer.

SIT.: In this revelation, which was given through Joseph Smith to the church in 1834, the Lord is rebuking the saints because of their lack of obedience. CON.: D & C 105:1-10.

( ) **7. D & C 90:36**

I, the Lord, will contend with Zion, and plead with her strong ones, and chasten her until she overcomes and is clean before me.

SIT.: This revelation was given to Joseph Smith in 1833. CON.: D & C 90:32-37.

( ) **8. Heb. 12:11**

No chastening for the present seemeth to be joyous, but grievous: nevertheless afterward it yieldeth the peaceable fruit of righteousness unto them which are exercised thereby.

SIT.: Paul is showing that the saints must be willing to accept chastening so that they will be able to partake of the Lord's holiness. CON.: Heb. 12:4-11.

( ) **9. D & C 122:7-8**

Know thou, my son, that all these things shall give thee experience, and shall be for thy good. The Son of Man hath descended below them all. Art thou greater than he?

SIT.: In this revelation, which was given to Joseph Smith in 1839, the Lord reviews many of the persecutions which Joseph has had to endure and may yet encounter, and counsels him to endure them faithfully. CON.: D & C 122:1-9.

( ) **10. D & C 101:3-5**

They shall be mine in that day when I shall come to make up my jewels. Therefore, they must needs be chastened and tried, even as Abraham, who was commanded to offer up his only son. For all those who will not endure chastening, but deny me, cannot be sanctified.

SIT.: In this revelation, which was given to Joseph Smith in 1833, the Lord reveals that he has allowed the saints in Jackson Co., Mo., to be afflicted because of their transgressions. CON.: D & C 101:1-9.

51. SEEK WISDOM

( ) **1. Jas. 3:17**
The wisdom that is from above is first pure, then peaceable, gentle, and easy to be intreated, full of mercy and good fruits, without partiality, and without hypocrisy.
> *SIT.: James is contrasting the nature of earthly wisdom and wisdom given through inspiration. CON.: Jas. 3:13-18.*

( ) **2. Prov. 1:7**
The fear of the LORD is the beginning of knowledge: but fools despise wisdom and instruction.
> *CON.: Prov. 1:1-9.*

( ) **3. Job 28:28**
The fear of the Lord, that is wisdom; and to depart from evil is understanding.
> *SIT.: After asking where shall wisdom be found, Job explains that God knows its source and then makes this statement.   CON.: Job 28:12-28. C.R.: Prov. 9:10.*

( ) **4. Prov. 4:7-8**
Wisdom is the principal thing; therefore get wisdom: and with all thy getting get understanding. Exalt her, and she shall promote thee: she shall bring thee to honour, when thou dost embrace her.
> *CON.: Prov. 4:1-13.*

( ) 5. Prov. 9:1, 4-5

Wisdom hath builded her house, she hath hewn out her seven pillars:...Whoso is simple, let him turn in hither: as for him that wanteth understanding, she saith to him, Come, eat of my bread, and drink of the wine which I have mingled.

CON.: Prov. 9:1-12.

( ) 6. Prov. 4:13

Take fast hold of instruction; let her not go: keep her; for she is thy life.

CON.: Prov. 4:1-13.

( ) 7. Prov. 10:1

A wise son maketh a glad father: but a foolish son is the heaviness of his mother.

( ) 8. Prov. 22:17

Bow down thine ear, and hear the words of the wise, and apply thine heart unto my knowledge.

( ) 9. Al. 32:23

[God] imparteth his word by angels unto men, yea, not only men but women also. Now this is not all; little children do have words given unto them many times which confound the wise and the learned.

SIT.: Alma is speaking of the nature of faith to the Zoramites. CON.: Al. 32:21-27.

( ) 10. Mt. 7:24

Whosoever heareth these sayings of mine, and doeth

them, I will liken him unto a wise man, which built
his house upon a rock.

SIT.: Jesus, in his Sermon on the Mount, *said
these words as he introduced the parable of the
house upon the rock. CON.: Mt. 7:24-27. C.R.:
3 Ne. 14:24-27.*

52. AID THE POOR AND AFFLICTED

( ) 1. **Gen. 4:9**

Am I my brother's keeper?

SIT.: These words were spoken by Cain to the Lord as the Lord asked where was Abel, whom Cain had just slain. CON.: Gen. 4:1-15.

( ) 2. **D & C 52:40**

Remember in all things the poor and the needy, the sick and the afflicted, for he that doeth not these things, the same is not my disciple.

SIT.: This revelation was given through Joseph Smith to elders of the church in 1831.

( ) 3. **D & C 88:123**

See that ye love one another; cease to be covetous; learn to impart one to another as the gospel requires.

SIT.: This revelation was given through Joseph Smith to the church in 1832.

( ) 4. **Jas. 1:27**

Pure religion and undefiled before God and the Father is this, To visit the fatherless and widows in their affliction, and to keep himself unspotted from the world.

SIT.: James is stressing the need to be doers of the word and not hearers only. CON.: Jas. 1:22-27.

( ) **5. Heb. 13:1-2**

Let brotherly love continue. Be not forgetful to
entertain strangers: for thereby some have enter-
tained angels unawares.

*SIT.: Paul is giving a series of diverse admoni-
tions.*

( ) **6. Acts 20:35**

Ye ought to support the weak, and to remember the
words of the Lord Jesus, how he said, It is more
blessed to give than to receive.

*SIT.: Paul, in his final charge to the elders at
Ephesus, said these words as he reminded them
of his labors to meet his own needs and the
needs of others. CON.: Acts 20:31-35.*

( ) **7. Mos. 4:24-25**

I say unto the poor, ye who have not and yet have
sufficient, that ye remain from day to day; I mean
all you who deny the beggar, because ye have not;
I would that ye say in your hearts that: I give not
because I have not, but if I had I would give. And
now, if ye say this in your hearts ye remain guilt-
less, otherwise ye are condemned; and your condemnation is just for ye covet that which ye have not
received.

*SIT.: King Benjamin is telling the people of
Zarahemla that they should be willing to give to
the poor because they are all beggars before
God. CON.: Mos. 4:16-26.*

( ) **8. D & C 81:5**

Be faithful; stand in the office which I have appointed unto you; succor the weak, lift up the hands which hang down, and strengthen the feeble knees.

SIT.: This revelation was given through Joseph Smith to Frederick G. Williams in 1832.

( ) **9. D & C 38:35**

They shall look to the poor and the needy, and administer to their relief that they shall not suffer; and send them forth to the place which I have commanded them.

SIT.: In this revelation, which was given to the church in 1831, the Lord commanded that men be appointed to look after the poor in the church as the saints in the eastern branches moved to the west. CON.: D & C 38:31-36.

( ) **10. 2 Cor. 1:4**

[God] comforteth us in all our tribulation, that we may be able to comfort them which are in any trouble, by the comfort wherewith we ourselves are comforted of God.

SIT.: Paul is praising God for aiding the saints in times of tribulation. CON.: 2 Cor. 1:3-7.

53. HAVE CHARITY

( ) **1. Col. 3:14**

Above all these things put on charity, which is the bond of perfectness.

SIT.: Paul has been listing various qualities which the saints should possess. CON.: Col. 3:12-16.

( ) **2. 1 Cor. 13:1-2**

Though I speak with the tongues of men and of angels, and have not charity, I am become as sounding brass, or a tinkling cymbal. And though I have the gift of prophecy, and understand all mysteries, and all knowledge; and though I have all faith, so that I could remove mountains, and have not charity, I am nothing.

( ) **3. 1 Cor. 13:3-4**

And though I bestow all my goods to feed the poor, and though I give my body to be burned, and have not charity, it profiteth me nothing. Charity suffereth long, and is kind; charity envieth not; charity vaunteth not itself, is not puffed up.

( ) **4. 1 Cor. 13:5-6**

Doth not behave itself unseemly, seeketh not her own, is not easily provoked, thinketh no evil; Rejoiceth not in iniquity, but rejoiceth in the truth.

( ) **5. 1 Cor. 13:7-8**

Beareth all things, believeth all things, hopeth all

things, endureth all things. Charity never faileth: but whether there be prophecies, they shall fail; whether there be tongues, they shall cease; whether there be knowledge, it shall vanish away.

SIT.: This is Paul's great exposition on the excellence of charity. CON.: 1 Cor. 13:1-13.

( ) **6. Moro. 10:20**

There must be faith; and if there must be faith there must also be hope; and if there must be hope there must also be charity.

( ) **7. Moro. 10:21**

And except ye have charity ye can in nowise be saved in the kingdom of God; neither can ye be saved in the kingdom of God if ye have not faith; neither can ye if ye have no hope.

SIT.: In his farewell to the Lamanites Moroni is saying that there are many spiritual gifts which will never cease except through the wickedness of men. CON.: Moro. 10:8-23.

( ) **8. Eth. 12:34**

I know that this love which thou hast had for the children of men is charity; wherefore, except men shall have charity they cannot inherit that place which thou hast prepared in the mansions of thy Father.

SIT.: Moroni is offering a prayer to the Lord concerning faith, hope, and charity. CON.: Eth. 12:29-35.

( ) **9. 2 Ne. 26:30**

The Lord God hath given a commandment that all
men should have charity, which charity is love. And
except they should have charity there were nothing.
Wherefore, if they should have charity they would
not suffer the laborer in Zion to perish.

SIT.:While prophesying concerning the last days,
Nephi tells of secret combinations and priest-
crafts and then warns that if they engage in these
things rather than have charity men will perish.
CON.: 2 Ne. 27:22-31.

( ) **10. Al. 7:24**

See that ye have faith, hope, and charity, and then
ye will always abound in good works.

SIT.: Alma is admonishing the saints in Gideon
to awaken to their duty to God. CON.: Al. 7:22-27.

See "Charity," *Gifts of The Spirit* pp. 317-324, for
further explanation on this subject.

54. NEED AND DESIRE FOR MISSIONARY WORK

( ) **1. D & C 6:3**

The field is white already to harvest; therefore, whoso desireth to reap, let him thrust in his sickle with his might, and reap while the day lasts, that he may treasure up for his soul everlasting salvation in the kingdom of God.

> *SIT.: This message was revealed repeatedly by the Lord to early church leaders. See D & C 4:4; 11:3; 12:3; 14:3; 33:3, 7; Jn. 4:35.*

( ) **2. D & C 6:4**

Yea, whosoever will thrust in his sickle and reap, the same is called of God.

> *C.R.: D & C 4:4; 11:4, 27; 12:4; 14:4; 31:5; 33:7.*

( ) **3. D & C 4:3**

If ye have desires to serve God ye are called to the work.

( ) **4. Al. 29:9**

I do not glory of myself, but I glory in that which the Lord hath commanded me; yea, and this is my glory, that perhaps I may be an instrument in the hands of God to bring some soul to repentance; and this is my joy.

> *SIT.: Alma said this as he expressed his great desire to cry repentance to the people. CON.: Al. 29:1-10.*

( ) **5. D & C 18:15**

If it so be that you should labor all your days in crying repentance unto this people, and bring, save it be one soul unto me, how great shall be your joy in the kingdom of my Father!

SIT.: This revelation was given to Joseph Smith, Oliver Cowdery, and David Whitmer, in 1829. CON.: D & C 18:10-16.

( ) **6. Jas. 5:20**

He which converteth the sinner from the error of his way shall save a soul from death, and shall hide a multitude of sins.

CON.: Jas. 5:19-20.

( ) **7. Mos. 28:3**

They were desirous that salvation should be declared to every creature, for they could not bear that any human soul should perish; yea, even the very thoughts that any soul should endure endless torment did cause them to quake and tremble.

SIT.: This is a description of the sons of Mosiah as they requested permission from their father to preach to the Lamanites in the land of Nephi. CON.: Mos. 28:1-8.

( ) **8. Mk. 16:15-16**

Go ye into all the world, and preach the gospel to every creature. He that believeth and is baptized shall be saved; but he that believeth not shall be damned.

SIT.: This was the commandment of the resur-
rected Christ to his eleven disciples just before
he ascended into heaven. CON.: Mk. 16:14-20.
C.R.: Mt. 28:16-20.

( ) **9. Al. 29:1**

O that I were an angel, and could have the wish of
mine heart, that I might go forth and speak with the
trump of God, with a voice to shake the earth, and
cry repentance unto every people!
SIT.: Alma was expressing his great desire to do
missionary work. CON.: Al. 29:1-10.

( ) **10. Jn. 21:17**

Feed my sheep.
SIT.: The resurrected Christ appeared to his
disciples at the sea of Tiberias (Galilee). There
he talked with Peter and repeatedly gave him
instruction to feed his sheep, or care for his
followers. CON.: Jn. 21:15-17.

See "Missionary Work Among the Gentiles," *Proph-*
ecy—Key To The Future, pp. 17-34, to learn of
scriptural prophecies concerning missionary work
in the last days.

55. QUALIFICATIONS OF MISSIONARIES

( ) 1. Al. 17:2, 3, 9   **The Missionary Preparation of the Sons of Mosiah:**

1. They had searched the scriptures diligently.
2. They had given themselves to much prayer, and fasting.
3. They had the spirit of prophecy, and the spirit of revelation.
4. When they taught, they taught with power and authority of God.
5. They sought to be an instrument in the hands of God to bring their brethren to the truth.
   CON.: Al. 17:1-12.

( ) 2. **D & C 4:5-6**

And faith, hope, charity and love, with an eye single to the glory of God, qualify him for the work. Remember faith, virtue, knowledge, temperance, patience, brotherly kindness, godliness, charity, humility, diligence.

> *SIT.: This classic revelation on labor in the Lord's kingdom was given through Joseph Smith to his father, Joseph Smith Sr., in 1829. The above is a list of the qualities which are to be possessed by anyone who thrusts in his sickle to labor with his might.*

( ) 3. **Al. 26:22**

He that repenteth and exerciseth faith, and bringeth forth good works, and prayeth continually without ceasing—unto such it is given to know the mysteries of God; yea, unto such it shall be given to reveal things which never have been revealed; yea, and it shall be given unto such to bring thousands of souls to repentance.

> *SIT.: This was spoken by Ammon while he boasted in the Lord of his many blessings. CON.: Al. 26:1-37.*

( ) **4. Hel. 3:35**

They did fast and pray oft, and did wax stronger and stronger in their humility, and firmer and firmer in the faith of Christ, unto the filling their souls with joy and consolation, yea, even to the purifying and the sanctification of their hearts, which sanctification cometh because of their yielding their hearts unto God.

> *SIT.: This is a description of the righteous portion of the church in an era when they were being persecuted by those of the church who were lifted up in pride. CON.: Hel. 3:33-36.*

( ) **5. Al. 38:11-12**

See that ye are not lifted up unto pride; yea, see that ye do not boast in your own wisdom, nor of your much strength. Use boldness, but not overbearance; and also see that ye bridle all your passions, that ye may be filled with love; see that ye refrain from idleness.

> *SIT.: This counsel was given by Alma to his missionary son Shiblon. CON.: Al. 38:10-15.*

( ) **6. 1 Ne. 13:37**

Blessed are they who shall seek to bring forth my
Zion at that day, for they shall have the gift and the
power of the Holy Ghost,...and whoso shall publish
peace, yea, tidings of great joy, how beautiful upon
the mountains shall they be.

> *SIT.: While prophesying of the coming forth of the
> Book of Mormon in the last days, Nephi cited the
> word of the Lord about those who labor in the ef-
> fort to bring forth Zion. CON.: 1 Ne. 13:35-42.
> C.R.: D & C 128:19; Is. 52:7; Ro. 10:15.*

( ) **7. D & C 84:43-44**

I give unto you a commandment to beware concerning
yourselves, to give diligent heed to the words of
eternal life. For you shall live by every word that
proceedeth forth from the mouth of God.

> *SIT.: This revelation was given through Joseph
> Smith to elders of the church in 1832. CON.:
> D & C 84:33-44.*

( ) **8. D & C 43:16**

Ye are to be taught from on high. Sanctify yourselves
and ye shall be endowed with power, that ye may
give even as I have spoken.

> *SIT.: This revelation was given through Joseph
> Smith to the church in 1831. CON.: D & C 43:8-16.*

( ) **9. Al. 8:10**

Alma labored much in the spirit, wrestling with God
in mighty prayer, that he would pour out his Spirit
upon the people who were in the city; that he would
also grant that he might baptize them unto repentance.

SIT.: This is a description of Alma as he attempted to labor among the wicked people of Ammonihah. CON.: Al. 8:7-26.

( ) **10. Al. 39:4**

Thou shouldst have tended to the ministry wherewith thou wast entrusted.

SIT.: This was a portion of the rebuke which Alma gave to his missionary son, Corianton. The son had left his missionary duties and had been tempted by the harlot Isabel. CON.: Al. 39:2-9.

See "Six Gifts of Self-Expression," *Gifts of The Spirit,* pp. 247-272, which explains the gifts of speaking, writing, translation, teaching, expounding the scriptures, and bearing testimony.

56. WHAT TO PREACH

( ) **1. Al. 37:33**

Preach unto them repentance, and faith on the Lord Jesus Christ; teach them to humble themselves and to be meek and lowly in heart; teach them to withstand every temptation of the devil, with their faith on the Lord Jesus Christ.

( ) **2. Al. 37:34**

Teach them to never be weary of good works, but to be meek and lowly in heart; for such shall find rest to their souls.

SIT.: This counsel was given by the prophet Alma to his son Helaman. CON.: Al. 37:33-37.

( ) **3. D & C 18:6**

The world is ripening in iniquity; and it must needs be that the children of men are stirred up unto repentance, both the Gentiles and also the house of Israel.

SIT.: This message was revealed to Joseph Smith, Oliver Cowdery and David Whitmer in 1829.

( ) **4. D & C 19:31**

Of tenets thou shalt not talk, but thou shalt declare repentance and faith on the Savior, and remission of sins by baptism, and by fire, yea, even the Holy Ghost.

SIT.: This commandment was revealed through Joseph Smith to Martin Harris. CON.: D & C 19. 29-32.

( ) **5. D & C 42:65**

Unto you it is given to know the mysteries of the kingdom, but unto the world it is not given to know them.

SIT.: This commandment was revealed through Joseph Smith to elders of the church in 1831.

( ) **6. D & C 52:36**

Let them labor with their families, declaring none other things than the prophets and apostles, that which they have seen and heard and most assuredly believe, that the prophecies may be fulfilled.

SIT.: This revelation was given through Joseph Smith concerning Joseph Wakefield and Solomon Humphrey, who were to serve as missionaries in the eastern states. CON.: D & C 52:35-36.

( ) **7. D & C 43:15**

Hearken ye elders of my church, whom I have appointed: Ye are not sent forth to be taught, but to teach the children of men the things which I have put into your hands by the power of my Spirit.

SIT.: This revelation was given to the elders of the church in 1831. They were commanded to be taught by each other and by their prophet rather than be taught by the precepts of men. CON.: D & C 43:8-16.

( ) **8. Is. 8:20**

To the law and to the testimony: if they speak not according to this word, it is because there is no light in them.

SIT.: This was the counsel Isaiah gave for contending with those who would consult with familiar (evil) spirits and wizards (mediums). CON.: Is. 8:16-22.

( ) **9. Job 38:2**

Who is this that darkeneth counsel by words without knowledge?

SIT.: These words were spoken by the LORD *to Job as a rebuke against the words of Elihu, who had just counselled Job. CON.: Job 38:1-7.*

( ) **10. D & C 14:8**

If you shall ask the Father in my name, in faith believing, you shall receive the Holy Ghost, which giveth utterance, that you may stand as a witness of the things of which you shall both hear and see, and also that you may declare repentance unto this generation.

SIT.: This promise was revealed through Joseph Smith to David Whitmer in 1829.

57. WARN OTHERS

( ) **1. D & C 38:41**

Let your preaching be the warning voice, every man
to his neighbor, in mildness and in meekness.

*SIT.: This revelation was given through Joseph
Smith to the church in 1831.*

( ) **2. D & C 88:81-82**

I sent you out to testify and warn the people, and it
becometh every man who hath been warned to warn
his neighbor. Therefore, they are left without excuse,
and their sins are upon their own heads.

*SIT.: This revelation was given through Joseph
Smith to the church in 1832. CON.: D & C 88:81-91.*

( ) **3. D & C 88:84**

Go forth among the Gentiles for the last time, as
many as the mouth of the Lord shall name, to bind
up the law and seal up the testimony, and to prepare
the saints for the hour of judgment which is to come.

*SIT.: This revelation was given through Joseph
Smith to the church in 1832. CON.: D & C 88:81-91.*

( ) **4. D & C 88:88**

After your testimony cometh wrath and indignation
upon the people.

*SIT.: This revelation was given through Joseph
Smith to the church in 1832. CON.: D & C 88:81-91.*

( ) **5. D & C 84:87**

I send you out to reprove the world of all their unrighteous deeds, and to teach them of a judgment which is to come.

SIT.: This revelation was given through Joseph Smith to elders of the church in 1832. CON.: D & C 84:77-97. C.R.: D & C 84:117; Moses 6:27.

( ) **6. D & C 63:57-58**

Those who desire in their hearts, in meekness, to warn sinners to repentance, let them be ordained unto this power. For this is a day of warning, and not a day of many words. For I, the Lord, am not to be mocked in the last days.

( ) **7. D & C 84:117**

Go ye forth as your circumstances shall permit, in your several callings, unto the great and notable cities and villages, reproving the world in righteousness of all their unrighteous and ungodly deeds, setting forth clearly and understandingly the desolation of abomination in the last days.

SIT.: This instruction was given to high priests and elders in a revelation through Joseph Smith in 1832. CON.: D & C 84:111-117.

( ) **8. Ezek. 3:17**

Son of man, I have made thee a watchman unto the house of Israel: therefore hear the word at my mouth, and give them warning from me.

( ) **9. Ezek. 3:18**

When I say unto the wicked, Thou shalt surely die; and thou givest him not warning, nor speakest to warn the wicked from his wicked way, to save his life; the same wicked man shall die in his iniquity; but his blood will I require at thine hand.

( ) 10. Ezek. 3:19

Yet if thou warn the wicked, and he turn not from his wickedness, nor from his wicked way, he shall die in his iniquity; but thou hast delivered thy soul.

SIT.: This was the word of the Lord unto Ezekiel as that prophet was called to labor among the Jews who had been carried into captivity by Babylonia. CON.: Ezek. 3:17-21. C.R. Ezek. 33:1-16.

58. COUNSEL TO MISSIONARIES

( ) 1. D & C 42:6

Ye shall go forth in the power of my Spirit, preaching my gospel, two by two, in my name, lifting up your voices as with the sound of a trump, declaring my word like unto angels of God.

SIT.: This commandment was revealed through Joseph Smith to elders of the church in 1831. CON.: D & C 42:4-17.

( ) 2. D & C 60:13

They have been sent to preach my gospel among the congregations of the wicked; wherefore, I give unto them a commandment, thus: Thou shalt not idle away thy time, neither shalt thou bury thy talent that it may not be known.

SIT.: This commandment was revealed through Joseph Smith to missionaries departing for their fields of labor in 1831. CON.: D & C 60:13-15.

( ) 3. D & C 75:3-4

It is my will that you should go forth and not tarry, neither be idle but labor with your might—Lifting up your voices as with the sound of a trump, proclaiming the truth according to the revelations and commandments which I have given you.

SIT.: This revelation was given through Joseph Smith to missionaries of the church in 1832. CON.: D & C 75:2-5.

( ) 4. 3 Ne. 11:29-30

He that hath the spirit of contention is not of me, but is of the devil, who is the father of contention, and he stirreth up the hearts of men to contend with anger, one with another. Behold, this is not my doctrine, to stir up the hearts of men with anger, one against another; but this is my doctrine, that such things should be done away.

SIT.: This instruction was given by the resurrected Christ as he appeared among the Nephites and Lamanites in the Americas. He was warning his disciples against allowing disputations on doctrine within the church. CON.: 3 Ne. 11:28-40.

( ) 5. D & C 75:27

Let them ask and they shall receive, knock and it shall be opened unto them, and be made known from on high, even by the Comforter, whither they shall go.

SIT.: This revelation was given through Joseph Smith to missionaries of the church in 1832. CON.: D & C 75:26-29.

( ) 6. D & C 68:3

This is the ensample unto them, that they shall speak as they are moved upon by the Holy Ghost.

SIT.: This example was given to all ordained members of the priesthood through Joseph Smith in 1831. CON.: D & C 68:2-6.

( ) 7. D & C 75:19

In whatsoever house ye enter, and they receive you, leave your blessing upon that house.

SIT.: This revelation was given through Joseph Smith to missionaries of the church in 1832. CON.: D & C 75:18-22.

( ) **8. D & C 99:4**

Whoso rejecteth you shall be rejected of my Father and his house; and you shall cleanse your feet in the secret places by the way for a testimony against them.

SIT.: This revelation was given through Joseph Smith to John Murdock, an early missionary, in 1833. C.R.: D & C 60:15; 75:20; 84:92-95; Mt. 10:14; Mk. 6:11; Lk. 9:5; 10:10-12; Acts 13:51.

( ) **9. D & C 84:80**

Any man that shall go and preach this gospel of the kingdom, and fail not to continue faithful in all things, shall not be weary in mind, neither darkened, neither in body, limb, nor joint; and a hair of his head shall not fall to the ground unnoticed. And they shall not go hungry, neither athirst.

SIT.: This revelation was given through Joseph Smith to elders of the church in 1832. CON.: D & C 84:77-97.

( ) **10. D & C 18:20-21**

Contend against no church, save it be the church of the devil. Take upon you the name of Christ, and speak the truth in soberness.

SIT.: This revelation was given to Joseph Smith, Oliver Cowdery, and David Whitmer in 1829. C.R.: D & C 68:1.

59. TESTIMONY

( ) 1. Mt. 16:16-17

Simon Peter answered and said, Thou art the Christ, the Son of the living God. And Jesus answered and said unto him, Blessed art thou, Simon Barjona: for flesh and blood hath not revealed it unto thee, but my Father which is in heaven.

SIT.: When Jesus came to the coasts of Caesarea he asked his disciples whom do men say that he is. After hearing several answers he asked Peter, "But whom say ye that I am?" CON.: Mt. 16: 13-20. C.R.: =Mk. 8:27-30; =Lk. 9:18-22.

( ) 2. Jn. 20:29

Thomas, because thou hast seen me, thou hast believed: blessed are they that have not seen, and yet have believed.

SIT.: The resurrected Christ had appeared to his disciples a week previous. Thomas had not been present, and he refused to believe his Lord was resurrected until he could see and feel him. Jesus appeared and had Thomas touch and view him. CON.: Jn. 20:19-29.

( ) 3. D & C 84:61

I will forgive you of your sins with this commandment—that you remain steadfast in your minds in solemnity and the spirit of prayer, in bearing testimony to all the world of those things which are communicated unto you.

SIT.: This commandment was revealed through

Joseph Smith to elders of the church in 1832. CON.: D & C 84:54-61.

( ) 4. D & C 62:3

Ye are blessed, for the testimony which ye have borne is recorded in heaven for the angels to look upon; and they rejoice over you, and your sins are forgiven you.

SIT.: This revelation was given through Joseph Smith to elders of the church in 1831.

( ) 5. D & C 58:47

Let them preach by the way, and bear testimony of the truth in all places, and call upon the rich, the high and the low, and the poor to repent.

SIT.: This revelation was given through Joseph Smith concerning missionaries from Jackson County, Mo., in 1831. CON.: D & C 58:46-48.

( ) 6. D & C 6:22-23

Cast your mind upon the night that you cried unto me in your heart, that you might know concerning the truth of these things. Did I not speak peace to your mind concerning the matter? What greater witness can you have than from God?

SIT.: This revelation was given through Joseph Smith to Oliver Cowdery in 1829. It had reference to an experience known only to Oliver Cowdery at the time. CON.: D & C 6:14-24.

( ) **7. 1 Jn. 5:9**

If we receive the witness of men, the witness of God is greater: for this is the witness of God which he hath testified of his Son.

CON.: 1 Jn. 5:6-12.

( ) **8. 1 Jn. 4:14-15**

We have seen and do testify that the Father sent the Son to be the Saviour of the world. Whosoever shall confess that Jesus is the Son of God, God dwelleth in him, and he in God.

CON.: 1 Jn. 4:13-16.

( ) **9. Acts 8:36-37**

The eunuch said, See, here is water; what doth hinder me to be baptized? And Philip said, If thou believest with all thine heart, thou mayest. And he answered and said, I believe that Jesus Christ is the Son of God.

SIT.: Philip had been directed by an angel and by the Spirit to preach to an Ethiopian eunuch. He explained the prophecies of Isaiah to the eunuch and taught him about Jesus. CON.: Acts 8:26-39.

( ) **10. D & C 50:21-22**

Why is it that ye cannot understand and know, that He that receiveth the word by the Spirit of truth receiveth it as it is preached by the Spirit of truth? Wherefore, he that preacheth and he that receiveth, understand one another, and both are edified and rejoice together.

SIT.: In this revelation the Lord is giving man aids for discerning between the different spirits on the earth.   CON.: D & C 50:10-34.   C.R.: 2 Ne. 33:1-2.

See "The Gift of Bearing Testimony," *Gifts of The Spirit*, pp. 268-272.

Contents of the companion volume

A GUIDE TO EFFECTIVE SCRIPTURE STUDY

Contents of the companion volume

THE PLAN OF SALVATION
and
THE FUTURE IN PROPHECY

The Plan of Salvation

Contents of the companion volume

COME UNTO CHRIST

Marriage and Family Living

Principles of Harmonious Living

A Godlike Character

REFERENCE INDEX

1:25	40		*Philippians*	
1:26-27	192		2:3-4	194
1:31	189		2:10-11	37
3:8-9	172		4:12-13	193
3:18-19	192			
8:5-6	30		*Colossians*	
9:24	173		1:9	190
10:1-4	36		2:12	157
13:1-2	205		3:14	205
13:3-4	205		3:16	188
13:5-6	205			
13:7-8	205		*I Thessalonians*	
14:12	186		3:13	37
14:26	188			
15:58	182		*2 Thessalonians*	
			2:3-4	82
2 Corinthians			3:13	181
1:4	204			
7:10	154		*I Timothy*	
8:3	181		3:2	123
8:12	187		3:8-9	123
9:6	172		4:1-3	84
13:1	100		4:12	183
			5:17	176
Galatians				
1:6-7	86		*2 Timothy*	
1:8-9	86		2:15	181
1:10	189		3:1-2, 5	83
5:25-26	193		3:15	15
6:9-10	172		3:16	15
Ephesians			*Titus*	
1:9-10	94		2:7-8	184
2:8-10	150		2:13	93
2:19-21	122			
3:14-15	27		*Hebrews*	
4:5	114		1:2-3	26
4:11	122		5:1	122
5:17	189		5:4	118
5:19	188		5:10	124
			10:24-25	185

ABOUT THE AUTHOR

Duane S. Crowther is well known as an author, scriptorian, theologian, and lecturer. He has a rich background of training and experience which well qualifies him to prepare this scripture guide series. *God and His Church, Come Unto Christ, The Plan of Salvation and The Future in Prophecy*, and *A Guide to Effective Scripture Study* are evidence of his penetrating knowledge of the scriptures.

Mr. Crowther graduated with high honors as a music major from Brigham Young University with a Bachelor of Arts degree, then remained to complete a Master of Arts degree with an Old Testament major and a minor in New Testament. He has also received extensive training on a Ph D level at the University of Utah and Utah State University.

In the professional life he has served four years as a teacher and principal in the LDS Seminary system. He has also taught music in the public schools and has taught extension courses for BYU and for the University of Utah. He is now engaged in independent activity as an author, researcher, lecturer, and publisher. Mr. Crowther has published five books prior to the release of this scripture series. They are: *Prophecy—Key to the Future, The Prophecies of Joseph Smith, Gifts of the Spirit, Prophets and Prophecies of the Old Testament*, and *Life Everlasting*. Few books have had a more profound influence upon recent Latter-day Saint thought than the works he has authored.

He has written and directed two outstanding patriotic productions which won national *Freedom Foundation at Valley Forge* medals for both the programs and the color television shows adapted from them.

Elder Crowther has rendered much service within the Church. He has completed both a stake and a foreign mission, has served as Mission Sunday School and MIA Supervisor, and has been a branch and district president. He has also served as a Sunday School and MIA Superintendent, an Elders Quorum President, and has filled numerous teaching assignments. As these books are being released Brother Crowther is an active member of the Church in the Bountiful, Utah area and is functioning as the stake drama director, regional coordinator for the BYU Admissions Advisor program, a Sunday School teacher, and a home teacher. He also serves as a baptizer in the Salt Lake Temple and is a frequent speaker at Sacrament Meetings, Firesides, and Stake Youth excursions.

He is married to the former Jean Decker and they are the parents of six children. His wife is also an author of books and articles.

Many honors have come to Elder Crowther. He is an Eagle Scout, a Master M-Man, and has been named a member of various honorary scholastic societies. He leads a busy, active life, but takes time for his hobbies, which include performing in several vocal groups, photography, and working with young people.

ORDER BLANK

The following publications may be ordered from your local Church bookstore or direct from *Horizon Publishers:*

GOD AND HIS CHURCH

The basic missionary and new member volume. (Contents are listed earlier in this book.)

Quantity
Ordered

—————— vinyl 6-ring looseleaf (pocket size) $4.50

—————— paperback (pocket size) $3.50

COME UNTO CHRIST

The personal development volume. (Contents are listed earlier in this book.)

—————— vinyl 6-ring looseleaf (pocket size) $4.50

—————— paperback (pocket size) $3.50

THE PLAN OF SALVATION and THE FUTURE IN PROPHECY

This volume describes God's eternal plan. (Contents are listed earlier in this book.)

—————— vinyl 6-ring looseleaf (pocket size) $4.50

—————— paperback (pocket size) $3.50

A GUIDE TO EFFECTIVE SCRIPTURE STUDY

This volume coordinates the series with indexes and a learning program and gives guides for scriptural understanding and interpretation. (Contents are listed earlier in this book.)

—————— vinyl 6-ring looseleaf (pocket size) $4.50

—————— paperback (pocket size) $3.50

DAILY CALENDAR AND
PLANNING GUIDE

_____	brown vinyl cover	$3.95
_____	black vinyl cover	$3.95

This attractive vest-pocket item combines maximum convenience with outstanding utility. Housed in a sturdy, heavy-duty, four-pocket cover of attractive brown or black vinyl are a year-long calendar (a month at a glance, with space to list appointments) and a month-long series of daily planning sheets. Each day has two pages with provision for effective planning from 6 a.m. to 10 p.m. Space is also provided each day for notes, for summarizing time spent, for financial items, etc. Each planning pad serves for a month and contains scripture passages for daily learning. Passages for each month are drawn from different books of the Bible. The cover is re-useable, and different refills will be available year to year. Each set contains a vinyl cover, a calendar for the current year, and twelve different planning guides—sufficient for the entire year. ＊＊＊＊

Please send the items checked to:

Name _____

Address _____

City _____ State _____ Zip _____

_____

BOOKS .... _____

HANDLING & MAILING (50¢) (for outside the
    continental US add sufficient to cover the additional postage) .... _____

SALES TAX (In Utah add 4½%).......... _____

TOTAL .... _____